DAILY GRAMS: Guided Review Aiding Mastery Skills

GRADE 5

Author: Wanda C. Phillips

Published by ISHA Enterprises, Inc.
Easy Grammar Systems™
Post Office Box 25970
Scottsdale, Arizona 85255
www.easygrammar.com
© 2002

DAILY GRAMS: GUIDED REVIEW AIDING MASTERY SKILLS - GRADE 5
may be reproduced by the purchaser for student use only. Permission is not granted for district-wide, school-wide, or system-wide use. Reproduction for any commercial use is forbidden. Copyrighted materials. All rights reserved. No part of this book may be reproduced, stored in a retrieval system, or transmitted in any form or by any means, electronic, mechanical, recording, or otherwise.

CAPITALIZATION
Content and Sequence
Grade 5

Numbers indicate DAYS (page numbers) on which that concept is reviewed.

ABBREVIATION: 14, 18, 26, 37, 114, 142

BRAND NAME: 31, 88, 122, 141

BUSINESS: 8, 19, 22, 24, 28, 31, 47, 51, 71, 74, 75, 101, 109, 113, 122, 125, 146

CLOSING of a LETTER: 15, 36, 79, 106, 115, 133, 163

CLUB/ORGANIZATION: 47, 49, 55, 89, 105, 135, 147, 150, 162, 177

DAY of the WEEK: 3, 15, 48, 105, 117, 151

ETHNIC GROUP: 21, 39, 48, 75, 90, 96, 108, 132, 163, 169, 174

FREEWAY/INTERSTATE/Etc.: 48, 71, 90, 98

FRIENDLY LETTER: 15, 36, 64, 79, 106, 115, 133, 139, 163

GALAXY: 106

GEOGRAPHIC PLACES:
    Bay: 72, 145
    Beach: 6
    Borough: 112
    Cape: 81
    Canyon: 2, 127
    Cave: 60
    Channel: 23
    Continent: 17, 40, 66, 81, 114, 128, 130, 175, 176
    Country: 7, 21, 30, 37, 38, 39, 46, 67, 97, 104, 161, 168, 172, 174, 176
    County: 131
    Dam: 160
    Desert: 167
    District: 57, 121
    Forest (National): 72
    Gulf: 69, 126
    Island(s): 20, 102
    Lake: 5, 53, 128
    Mountain(s): 7, 25, 40, 62, 128, 129, 161, 176
    Ocean: 102
    Park: 3, 94, 117
    Park (National): 11, 18, 25, 173
    Region of Country: 13, 44, 45, 73, 115, 156
    Region of World: 99, 105
    River: 33, 44, 112, 160, 161
    Sea: 62, 99
    Square: 10, 95
    State: 1, 4, 6, 18, 24, 25, 33, 34, 52, 53, 62, 64, 69, 72, 77, 79, 86, 102, 106, 108, 115, 126, 127, 129, 133, 139, 144, 153, 160, 163, 167, 173
    Strait: 77
    Territory: 138
    Town/City: 1, 16, 33, 34, 52, 57, 61, 64, 69, 71, 77, 79, 106, 115, 126, 127, 129, 133, 139, 144, 153, 160, 163, 167, 173
    Valley: 131, 138
    Waterfall: 17

GOVERNMENT: 37

GOVERNMENT BODY or AGENCY: 56, 137, 155, 157

GREETING of a FRIENDLY LETTER: 15, 36, 64, 79, 107, 115, 133, 139, 163

HISTORICAL DOCUMENT: 14, 54, 107, 158, 161

HISTORICAL EVENT: 42, 83, 85, 96, 124, 137, 175

HOLIDAY/SPECIAL DAY: 6, 13, 20, 27, 55, 88, 143, 148, 162, 165, 177, 180

LANGUAGE: 30, 45, 97

MONTH: 2, 9, 17, 64, 79, 87, 106, 107, 115, 117, 133, 136, 139, 143, 163, 166

NAMES of PEOPLE: 1, 2, 4, 8, 9, 15, 16, 18, 19, 20-23, 24, 26, 32, 34-36, 39, 43, 44, 49, 54, 58, 60, 64, 66, 67, 73, 74, 76, 78, 79, 81, 84-86, 88, 94, 100, 103, 104, 106, 110, 115, 120, 121, 127, 131, 133, 135, 137-139, 141, 143, 144, 148, 150, 153, 155, 156, 158, 161, 163, 165-168, 170, 172, 179

NATIONALITY: 23, 83, 119, 138, 142, 150, 170, 172, 174, 175

OUTLINE: 41, 63, 70, 91, 116, 134, 164

PERIOD of TIME: 46, 76, 114, 179

POETRY (First Word of a Line): 59, 68, 92, 140, 149, 178

POLITICAL PARTY or MEMBER: 50, 74, 103, 121, 136, 168

PRONOUN, I: 6, 12, 28, 31, 36, 130, 132, 141, 150

PROPER ADJECTIVE: 13, 16, 22, 23, 35, 43, 48, 66, 73, 75, 84, 89, 95, 96, 100, 103, 111, 113, 119, 124, 125, 127, 130, 137, 138, 142, 146, 148, 165, 170, 179, 180

QUOTATION:
    First Word: 35, 43, 60, 66, 94, 100, 103, 153, 155, 156
    In Split Quotation: 127, 131, 179

RELIGION: 80, 110, 169, 174

SCHOOL/COLLEGE: 9, 27, 86, 146

SENTENCE, FIRST WORD: 1-28, 30-40, 42-58, 60-62, 66, 67, 69, 71-81, 83-90, 94-115, 117-122, 124-132, 133, 135-138, 141-148, 150-151, 153-163, 165-170, 172-177, 179, 180

SPECIAL EVENT: 26, 34, 153, 154, 169

STREET/LANE/AVENUE/Etc.: 3, 51, 57, 64, 79, 95, 98, 106, 109, 115, 122, 133, 139, 144, 163

STRUCTURES:
Castle: 128	Fort: 119, 172	Military Base: 60
Center: 52, 87, 180	House: 10, 158	Museum: 119, 163, 166
Church/Temple/Etc.: 32, 38	Lighthouse: 145	Palace: 84
Coliseum: 118	Mansion: 112	Ranch: 173
Farm: 111	Memorial: 57	Stadium/Ballpark: 98
		Tunnel: 52

TITLE in PLACE of a NAME: 24, 45, 61, 88, 109

TITLE of BOOKS and OTHER WORKS: 12, 29, 58, 65, 78, 82, 93, 122, 123, 132, 147, 152, 159, 171, 177

TITLE of SHIP, PLANE, or TRAIN: 43, 61, 67

TITLE with a NAME (*Captain, Mrs., etc.*): 2, 8, 15, 18, 20, 28, 44, 49, 50, 66, 67, 74, 79, 84, 88, 107, 119, 122, 133, 138, 150, 151, 155, 159, 165, 179

DO NOT CAPITALIZE:
    Animals: 15, 35, 100, 111, 130

Career Choices: 15, 19, 23, 26, 78, 81, 84, 86, 103, 126, 135, 138, 142, 154
Directions: 51, 98, 109
Diseases: 73, 87, 141
Foods: 13, 89, 101, 125
Musical Instruments: 165
School Subjects: 11, 39, 58, 106, 110, 120, 130, 150, 170
Seasons: 18, 24, 119, 131, 146, 148, 163

PUNCTUATION
Content and Sequence
Grade 5

Numbers indicate DAYS (page numbers) on which that concept is reviewed.

APOSTROPHE:
    Contraction: 3, 6, 11, 12, 13, 15, 21, 34, 36, 41-44, 49, 54, 62, 63, 66, 68, 71, 79, 81, 85-88, 94-97, 102, 107, 111, 112, 114, 118, 128, 131, 134, 141, 145, 148, 151, 161, 165, 167, 171, 172
    OmittedLetter(s)/Number(s): 18, 66, 148, 172
    Plural Possessive: 32, 38, 56, 57, 72, 76, 93, 98, 102, 105, 120, 121, 134, 137, 144, 154, 173, 180
    Singular Possessive: 1, 7, 20, 27, 36, 39, 48, 49, 51, 59, 60, 62, 67, 69, 78, 80, 82, 96, 98, 101, 111, 113, 117, 122, 124, 125, 128, 138, 146, 156, 166, 167, 168, 172

COLON:
    List - Vertical and Within Sentence: 5, 26, 53, 54, 58, 85, 89, 132, 169
    Time: 1, 15, 19, 115, 156, 161

COMMA:
    Address Within Sentence *(I live at 1 Lu Lane, Reno, Nevada.:* 4, 29, 57, 59, 116, 154, 166
    Adjective Phrase – Introductory *(Hot and dry,):* 129, 135
    Adjectives – Two Descriptive *(long, cold winter):* 20, 45, 73, 94, 109, 122, 123, 126, 133, 136, 165, 168
    Appositive: 39, 51, 67, 84, 120, 136, 139, 143, 156, 164, 168, 178
    Closing of a Letter: 31, 44, 61, 83, 104, 114, 121, 145, 163, 165, 172
    Compound Sentence: 125, 166
    Date *(January 1, 2000):* 7, 24, 31, 61, 80, 83, 104, 114, 121, 134, 145, 157, 163, 165, 172
    Date *(Monday, January 1):* 15, 31, 64, 72, 74, 80, 157, 172, 180
    Greeting of a Friendly letter: 6, 24, 31, 44, 61, 80, 83, 104, 114, 121, 145, 163, 165, 172
    Interrupter: 22, 43, 58, 71, 72, 74, 86, 89, 100, 111, 128, 160, 171, 173, 177
    Introductory Word(s): 3, 12, 21, 34, 36, 44, 64, 66, 68, 86, 88, 95, 126, 134, 158, 167, 173
    Inverted Name: 21, 60, 88, 128, 152
    Items in a Series: 2, 5, 25, 28, 34, 50, 54, 58, 83, 85, 89, 98, 104, 106, 124, 132, 142, 143, 154, 160, 169
    Noun of Direct Address: 10, 18, 19, 35, 63, 66, 71, 94, 97, 112, 126, 149, 158, 159, 161, 167
    Participial Phrase – Introductory: 82, 133, 142, 146, 147
    Prepositional phrase – Introductory: 69, 78, 91, 93, 117, 144, 161
    Quotation Marks:
        After Name of Person Speaking *(Tate said,):* 17, 42, 47, 49, 52, 62, 63, 75, 90, 95, 96, 99, 115, 118, 137, 157, 171, 176, 178
        Within a Quotation *("I like you," said Bob.):* 11, 32, 52, 56, 68, 86, 87, 90, 97, 99, 115, 157, 176-178
    Title After a Name *(Juan Lee, M.D, is here.):* 48, 76, 105, 144, 164
    Town/City with Country *(Paris, France):* 44, 47, 101, 114, 138
    Town/City with State *(Lithonia, GA):* 9, 24, 33, 41, 48, 61, 81, 83, 91, 92, 104, 109, 116, 121, 145, 163, 165
    Town/City with State/Country + Sentence *(Lisbon, Portugal, is lovely.):* 81, 101, 113, 118, 119, 138, 159, 166, 176

DASH: 73, 174, 175

EXCLAMATION POINT:
    Exclamatory Sentence: 13, 23, 46, 52, 75, 111, 166
    Interjection: 13, 46, 75, 166

HYPHEN:
    Closely related words: 9, 10, 11, 36, 38, 45, 68, 69, 79, 98, 104, 122, 126, 138, 143, 177
    Divided word at end of sentence: 146, 169
    Fraction: 35, 100, 132, 169
    Number: 12, 41, 96, 119, 134, 137, 165

PARENTHESES: 73, 174, 175

PERIOD:
    Abbreviation: 4, 9, 14, 15, 18, 19, 25, 27, 33, 40, 44, 48, 51, 57, 64, 70, 76, 87, 88, 90-92, 99, 102, 105, 109, 110, 112, 116, 117, 120-122, 131, 134, 137, 140, 144, 145, 152, 154, 156, 157, 163, 165, 170, 172
    Initials: 9, 27, 51, 76, 92, 99, 11, 17, 166
    Outline: 8, 37, 65, 108, 162
    Sentence Ending: 1-7, 9, 11, 12, 15, 17, 20-23, 25, 27-29, 31-34, 38, 39, 41, 43-47, 50-54, 56, 58-61, 64, 66-69, 71-74, 76, 78, 80-83, 86-90, 93-95, 97-102, 104-107, 109, 111-117, 119-126, 128, 129, 131-139, 141-148, 151, 152, 154, 156-161, 163-169, 171-177

PUNCTUATION Used in a Friendly Letter: 6, 24, 31, 44, 61, 80, 83, 104, 114, 121, 145, 163, 165, 172

QUESTON MARK: 10, 18, 19, 35, 36, 42, 49, 57, 62, 63, 84, 85, 96, 106, 112, 118, 149, 159, 175

QUOTATION MARKS:
    Direct Quotation:
        Occurring at Beginning (*"Go!" said Toni.*): 11, 23, 32, 46, 52, 56, 68, 86, 87, 97, 106, 111, 112, 159, 177
        Occurring at End (*Toni yelled, "Go!"*): 17, 42, 47, 49, 62, 63, 75, 95, 96, 118, 137, 171
        Split: 90, 99, 115, 157, 176, 178
    Title:
        Article: 30, 77, 127, 153, 155
        Chapter: 130, 175
        Essay: 179
        Nursery Rhyme: 153
        Poem: 16, 103, 130
        Story: 103, 127

SEMICOLON: 131, 141, 148, 151, 158, 180

UNDERLINING:
    Name of Ship/Plane/Train: 127, 153, 179
    Title:
        Book: 16, 77, 114, 123, 147, 150, 155
        Magazine: 77, 130
        Movie: 30, 103, 174, 179
        Newspaper: 55
        Television Show: 150, 155

Note: Concepts may also be included within other headings. For example, interjections, with obvious use of exclamation points, will be encountered under "Grammar and Other Concepts" on days *23, 87, 106, 114, 136,* and *163*. These page numbers have not been included in this sequence.

GRAMMAR AND OTHER CONCEPTS
Content and Sequence
Grade 5

Numbers indicate DAYS (page numbers) on which that concept is reviewed.

ADJECTIVES:
- Adjective or Adverb: 20, 36, 37, 40, 49, 53, 54, 62, 74, 75, 91, 97, 100, 121, 125, 130, 148, 150, 160, 175
- Adjective or Pronoun: 98, 124, 139, 153
- Degrees: 28, 56, 58, 78, 107, 136, 149, 165, 178
- Descriptive: 11, 27, 51, 76, 122, 151
- Identification – descriptive and limiting: 154, 166
- Predicate Adjectives: 49, 54
- Proper Adjectives: 101, 132, 162

ADVERBS:
- Adverb or Adjective: 20, 36, 37, 40, 49, 53, 54, 62, 74, 75, 91, 97, 100, 121, 125, 130, 148, 150, 160, 175
- Degrees: 15, 35, 58, 88, 117, 146, 156, 172
- Double Negatives: 92, 99, 143, 168
- How: 3, 23, 31, 50, 52, 69, 89, 131, 141, 161
- To What Extent: 65, 72, 81, 141, 161
- Use of Well: 20, 23, 36, 37, 40, 53, 75, 100, 121, 148, 175
- When: 1, 31, 52, 89, 110, 141, 161
- Where: 6, 26, 52, 110, 131, 141, 161

ANALOGIES: 1-4, 6, 8-10, 12, 14, 18, 20, 22, 24, 25, 28-36, 39-48, 52-56, 59, 60, 64-68. 70-73, 76, 80-82, 86-96, 100-105, 107, 108, 110-112, 115-121, 123, 127-130, 132, 133, 135, 136, 138, 139, 141, 144-148, 150-152, 155-157, 159, 160-162, 164, 166, 169, 170, 172, 173, 175, 176, 178, 180

CLAUSES (Independent/Dependent): 8, 71, 84, 94, 129, 159

CONJUNCTIONS: 9, 13, 42, 69, 87, 108, 136, 162

DICTIONARY SKILLS:
- Alphabetizing: 6, 33, 61, 86, 124, 134, 169
- Guide Words: 46, 73, 94, 123, 150, 172

DIFFICULT WORDS:
- Can/May: 13, 43, 68, 102
- They're/Their/There: 41, 43, 68, 102, 120
- To/Two/Too: 18, 43, 68, 102, 120
- You're/Your: 117

FRIENDLY LETTERS:
- Envelopes: 42, 60, 91, 118, 143, 157, 174, 176
- Letter Parts: 24, 44, 61, 79, 106, 115, 139, 145, 163, 168, 176

INTERJECTIONS: 23, 87, 106, 114, 136, 163

NOUNS:
- Abstract/Concrete: 4, 34, 64, 92, 118, 145, 170
- Common/Proper: 7, 8, 29, 47, 55, 80, 108, 137, 166
- Direct Objects: 86, 93, 104, 112, 113, 142, 153, 167, 180
- Identification: 1, 16, 39, 67, 95, 116, 121, 144, 177
- Indirect Object: 86, 104, 112, 153, 180
- Plurals: 17, 25, 31, 44, 57, 66, 89, 99, 109, 115, 128, 152, 173
- Possessives: 21, 65, 85, 113, 127, 130, 140, 142, 155, 158, 169, 174

PHRASES/CLAUSES: 19, 48, 56, 70, 95, 109, 132, 140, 157, 171

PREFIXES/ROOTS/SUFFIXES: 12, 16, 20, 29, 38, 40, 48, 49, 59, 67, 77, 85, 88, 90, 97, 111, 119. 126, 131, 137, 147, 155, 156, 164, 173, 177

PREPOSITIONS:
   Identification of Prepositional Phrases: 3, 14, 21, 34, 79, 80
   Object(s) of the Preposition: 21, 34, 80, 133

PRONOUNS:
   Nominative/Objective: 5, 12, 28, 30, 43, 53, 54, 63, 70, 83, 116, 138, 147, 160, 179
      Used as Object: 12, 30, 43, 63, 70, 116, 160, 179
      Used as Subject: 5, 12, 28, 30, 147
   Possessives: 82, 102
   Reflexive: 96, 112, 126, 154
   Use of We/Us (Beside a Noun): 53, 54, 83, 110, 138

SENTENCE COMBINING: 1-180

SENTENCE TYPES: 2, 9, 10, 24, 35, 38, 57, 82, 83, 103, 107, 119, 135, 138, 159, 167, 175

SENTENCES/FRAGMENTS/RUN-ONS: 32, 45, 64, 87, 105, 128, 146, 161, 180

SIMPLE/COMPOUND/COMPLEX SENTENCES: 61, 69, 97, 106, 122, 125, 126, 149, 154, 179

SPELLING: 5, 7, 11, 13, 15-17, 21, 23, 26, 27, 37, 38, 49-51, 57, 58, 62, 63, 74, 75, 77-79, 83-85, 98, 99, 109, 113, 114, 124, 131, 134, 137, 140, 142, 143, 153, 158, 163, 165, 167, 168, 171, 174, 177

SUBJECT/VERB AGREEMENT: 4, 8, 38, 60, 66, 71, 90, 117, 122, 127, 141, 170

SUBJECT and VERB/VERB PHRASE IDENTIFICATION: 2, 10, 22, 25, 36, 37, 45, 46, 51, 59, 72-74, 79, 93, 101, 104, 113, 133, 135, 142, 153, 158, 167, 180

SYNONYMS/ANTONYMS/HOMONYMS: 7, 22, 47, 76, 100, 129, 148, 165, 176

VERBS:
   Contractions: 5, 32, 52, 75, 81, 98, 103, 125, 152
   Compound: 37, 74, 101, 104, 158
   Helping Verbs/Verb Phrases: 10, 11, 15, 17, 26, 77, 114, 144
   Helping Verb or Main Verb: 17, 26, 50
   May or Can: 13, 41, 43, 68, 102
   Past Participle Construction of Irregular Verbs: 14, 19, 39, 62, 68, 84, 96, 111, 134, 151, 171, 178
   Regular or Irregular: 33, 63, 93, 120
   Sit/Sit and Lie/Lay: 18, 68
   Subject/Verb Agreement: 4, 8, 38, 60, 66, 71, 90, 117, 122, 127, 141, 170
   Subject/Verb Identification: 2, 10, 22, 25, 36, 37, 45, 46, 51, 59, 72-74, 79, 93, 101, 104, 113, 133, 135, 142, 153, 158, 167, 180
   Tenses: 27, 30, 55, 78, 105, 123, 149, 164, 179

The purpose of **DAILY GRAMS: GUIDED REVIEW AIDING MASTERY SKILLS - GRADE 5** is to provide students with **daily** review of their language. Review of concepts helps to promote **mastery learning.**

This particular text offers more "teaching" than some *Daily Grams* books. However, *this text is not a teaching text;* it has been specifically designed for review. As in other *Daily Grams* texts, concepts are usually repeated within twenty-five to thirty days.

FORMAT

Note that each page is set up in this manner:

1. Sentence #1 always contains **capitalization**.

2. In sentence #2, students insert needed **punctuation**. You may want students to write this sentence, adding proper punctuation.

3. Numbers 3 and 4 address **general concepts**. You may wish to replace one of these items with material you are currently studying, especially if the concept provided has not yet been introduced.

4. Analogies, spelling rules, and compound/complex sentences are introduced and reviewed in #5.

5. Number 6 is always a **sentence combining**. Using sentences given, students will write a more intricate sentence. This helps students to develop higher levels of writing. If you feel that the sentences given are too difficult, simply delete parts or replace them.

Note: An excellent teaching text for this level is **Easy Grammar: Grades 5 and 6**. To teach higher level sentence structures, **Easy Writing** is suggested. See the back of this text.

DAILY GRAMS: GUIDED REVIEW AIDING MASTERY SKILLS - GRADE 5

is designed as a guided review. There are 180 "GRAMS" in this book, one review per teaching day. **DAILY GRAMS** will take approximately **10 minutes** total time; this includes both completing and grading. (Do not be concerned if this takes slightly longer.)

PROCEDURE

1. Students should be **trained** to do "GRAMS" immediately upon entering the classroom. Therefore, "GRAMS" should be copied, written on the chalkboard, or placed on a transparency for use with an overhead projector. (The projector may need to be adjusted to enlarge the print.)

2. Students will finish at different rates. Two ideas are suggested:

    A. Students read when finished.

    B. Students write in daily journals.

3. Go over the answers orally as a class. Discuss answers. (Examples: Why is *Hispanic* capitalized? What is the rule for showing possession with any singular noun?)

4. In making students accountable for this type of activity, you may wish to take a quiz grade occasionally.

SUGGESTIONS

1. Make transparencies and file them. These can be used each year. Simply draw that day's "GRAMS" from your file.

2. You may choose to purchase a **workbook** for each student or to make copies for each student. A transparency is still needed. Students usually learn more by seeing the answers.

3. Allow students to use a dictionary, if necessary, to complete analogies.

4. Solicit as much student response as possible. Keep the lesson lively!

5. If possible, allow students to write sentence combinings on the board. Use this for class "editing" and **praise**!

6. As one progresses through this book, some of the sentence combinings become longer and more complex. This may necessitate an adaptation to your own teaching style and to your students' needs.

Note: Student **workbooks** are available and will save you valuable time. These contain the same daily reviews as the teacher text. The introductory pages and the answers are not included in the workbooks.

DAY 1

CAPITALIZATION:

1. is jane's family going to anchorage, alaska, this year?

PUNCTUATION:

2. Tammys dad left at 1 30 in the afternoon

PARTS OF SPEECH: NOUNS
   A noun names a person, a place, a thing, or an idea.
   Circle any nouns:

3. Sharon bought an old sofa for her apartment.

PARTS OF SPEECH: ADVERBS
   Circle any adverbs that tell *when*:

4. We are going today or tomorrow.

ANALOGIES:
   Analogies show relationships. First, determine how the first two words are related. Then, look at the third word and possible answers. Choose the answer that has the same relationship to the third word.
   The first two words (set) may be synonyms (have similar meanings).
   Example: Mad is to angry as frequent is to _____.
              (a) always   (b) furious   **(c) often**   (d) infrequent
   Analogies may also be written in this manner:
   Mad : angry :: frequent : _____.
   (a) always   (b) furious   **(c) often**   (d) infrequent

   Circle the correct answer:

5. large : enormous :: calm : _____
   (a) stormy   (b) upset   (c) peaceful   (d) preoccupied

SENTENCE COMBINING:

6. The pot is made of clay.
   The pot is filled with tulips.
   The tulips are yellow.

_____

_____

DAY 2

CAPITALIZATION:

1. in september, mr. and mrs. pino will visit the grand canyon.

PUNCTUATION:

2. That plant is tall leafy and healthy

SUBJECT/VERB:

The subject of a sentence tells *who* or *what* the sentence is about.
The verb tells what *is (was)* or what *happens (happened)*.

Note: Prepositional phrases usually aren't the subject or the verb.
Deleting them makes finding the subject and verb easier.
Example: Cal was ~~on the phone~~ ~~with his best friend~~.

Underline the subject once and the verb twice:

3. We laughed about the scar on my toe.

SENTENCE TYPES:

A declarative sentence makes a statement.

Write a declarative sentence about your shoe:

4. _____

ANALOGIES:

Circle the correct answer:

5. smart : intelligent :: lives : _____
   (a) dwellings   (b) resides   (c) rural   (d) packs

SENTENCE COMBINING:

6. Kim's Aunt is a dentist.
   Kim's aunt lives in Virginia Beach.

_____

_____

DAY 3

CAPITALIZATION:

1. last saturday we went to riverside park on cherry lane.
   (Corrections marked: L, S, R, P, C, L)

PUNCTUATION:

2. No͵We can't follow you!

PARTS OF SPEECH: PREPOSITIONS

Prepositional phrases begin with a preposition and end with a noun or a pronoun (such as *me, him, her, us,* or *them.*) Commonly used prepositions are *to, for, from, in, into, on,* and *with.*

Circle any prepositional phrases:

3. Come (with) us.

PARTS OF SPEECH: ADVERBS

Circle any adverbs that tell *how:*

4. They skate (fast).

ANALOGIES:

Circle the correct answer:

5. tasty : delicious :: tardy : _____
   (a) late   (b) naughty   (c) bell   (d) tired

SENTENCE COMBINING:

6. Their father is a salesman.
   Their grandfather is a salesman.

   Their father & grandfath are salesmen.

DAY 4

CAPITALIZATION:

1. is thomas jefferson's home located in virginia?

PUNCTUATION:

2. Their new address is 9400 N Offenhauser Drive Flagstaff Arizona   86004

SUBJECT/VERB:
Underline the subject; circle the verb that agrees with the subject:

3. Dorita (has, have) a new baby brother.

PARTS OF SPEECH: NOUNS
A concrete noun names a real thing.   Example: milk
An abstract nouns names an idea.   Example: truth

Write C if the noun is concrete; write A if the noun is abstract:

4. A. _____ magnet   B. _____ tower   C. _____ trust

SPELLING:
A word may end with a single consonant + e. A word ending with consonant + e usually drops that final e when adding a suffix (ending) that begins with a VOWEL. The e is not dropped if the suffix begins with a consonant.

   Examples: time + ing = tim**ing**   time + less = tim**e**less

Write the correct spelling of these words:

5. A. frame + ed - _____
   B. price + ing - _____
   C. price + less - _____

SENTENCE COMBINING:

6. His cousin is on a baseball team.
   His cousin plays third base.

_____

_____

DAY 5

CAPITALIZATION:

1. my grandfather's favorite place is wood's canyon lake.
   (M, W, C, L capitalized)

PUNCTUATION:

2. I need the following:raisins,peanuts, and coconut.

PARTS OF SPEECH: VERBS
Write the contraction:

3. A. who is - who's   D. did not - didn't
   B. have not - haven't E. I am - I'm
   C. we are - we're   F. I have - I've

PARTS OF SPEECH: PRONOUNS
Circle the correct answer:

4. (**Jim and I**, Me and Jim, Jim and me) found several deer paths.

SPELLING:
Write the correct spelling of these words:

5. A. use + ing - using
   B. use + ful - useful
   C. lease + ed - leased

SENTENCE COMBINING:

6. Maria called to her puppy.
   She held out her arms.

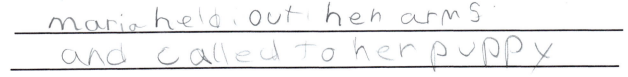

Maria held out her arms and called to her puppy

DAY 6

CAPITALIZATION:

1. on washington's birthday, i went to newport beach in california.

PUNCTUATION:

2. Dear Anna

   Ill meet you by the fountain

   Pedro

PARTS OF SPEECH: ADVERBS
Circle any adverbs that tell *where*:

3. The mouse scampered here and there.

DICTIONARY SKILLS: ALPHABETIZING
Write these words in alphabetical order:

4. offer   pioneer   noodle   manner   onion   nerve

ANALOGIES:
The first two words of an analogy may be antonyms (opposites). Again, look at your third word; your answer must have an opposite meaning of the third word.

Example: Stay : leave :: quiet : _____.
   (a) quite   **(b) noisy**   (c) peacefu   (d) dreams

Circle the correct answer:

5. laugh : cry :: deep : _____
   (a) river   (b) depend   (c) shallow   (d) dry

SENTENCE COMBINING:

6. Allie's hair is brown.
   Allie's hair has blonde streaks in it.
   Allie's hair is curly.

_____

_____

DAY 9

CAPITALIZATION:

1. during the first week of september, matt attended park meadows school.

PUNCTUATION:

2. Capt C L Linski lives in a two story townhouse in Hollywood California

SENTENCE TYPES:
An interrogative sentence asks a question. It expresses a complete thought and ends with a question mark.
Write an interrogative sentence:

3. _____

PARTS OF SPEECH: CONJUNCTIONS
Conjunctions are joining words.
Unscramble these commonly used conjunctions:

4. A. ro - _____   B. nda - _____   C. btu - _____

ANALOGIES:
The first two words of an analogy may be antonyms (opposites). Then, the third word and the answer must also be opposites.

Example: enter : exit :: punish : _____
(a) cry   **(b) reward**   (c) discipline   (d) scold

Enter is the opposite of *exit*; the opposite of *punish* is *reward*.

Circle the correct answer:

5. bold : timid :: narrow : _____
(a) stingy   (b) decrease   (c) limited   (d) broad

SENTENCE COMBINING:

6. Sponges have no tissue.
Sponges have no organs.

_____

_____

DAY 10

CAPITALIZATION:

1. the rossen house at heritage square is a famous historical building.

PUNCTUATION:
A noun of direct address is used to speak to someone.
If the noun of direct address is the first word, place a comma after it.
   Example: *Marlo,* may I help you?
If the noun of direct address is the last word, place a comma before it.
   Example: May I help you, *Marlo*?
If the noun of direct address is anywhere within the sentence, place a comma before it and a comma after it.
   Example: May I, *Marlo,* go with you?

2. Brian will you make strawberry filled pancakes for breakfast

SENTENCE TYPES:
Write an interrogative sentence:

3. _____

PARTS OF SPEECH: VERBS
A verb may be one word: Example: Tate <u>kicked</u> the ball.
A verb phrase consists of more than one word.
   Verb phrase = helping verb(s) + main verb
      Example: Jonah <u>had planned</u> a party for his parents.

Underline the subject once and the verb phrase twice:

4. Several speakers have presented their ideas.

ANALOGIES:
Circle the correct answer:

5. always : never :: partially : _____
   (a) closely   (b) recently   (c) completely   (d) practically

SENTENCE COMBINING:

6. Leeches are worms.
   They have suckers on both ends.

DAY 11

CAPITALIZATION:

1. we read about zion national park in our social studies class.

PUNCTUATION:

2. Im buying a three wheeled bike said Nana

PARTS OF SPEECH: ADJECTIVES
   Many adjectives are descriptive adjectives.
   Write a descriptive adjective; draw an arrow to the word it describes:

3. A _____ squirrel dashed up the _____ tree.

PARTS OF SPEECH: VERBS
   There are twenty-three helping (auxiliary) verbs.
   Unscramble these nine helping verbs:

4. A. od - _____   D. sha - _____   G. mya - _____
   B. sode - _____ E. veah - _____   H. gimht - _____
   C. ddi - _____   F. adh - _____   I. utsm - _____

SPELLING:
   Write the correct spelling of these words:

5. A. digest + ed - _____
   B. amuse + ing - _____
   C. brave + ly - _____

SENTENCE COMBINING:

6. The pie is peach.
   The pie is flaky.
   The pie is moist.

_____

_____

DAY 12

CAPITALIZATION:

1. i watched a movie entitled <u>the ten commandments</u>.

PUNCTUATION:

2. Yes hes fifty two years old today

PREFIXES/ROOTS/SUFFIXES:
    re + do + ing = redoing
  prefix   root   suffix

Five prefixes that are commonly used to express *not*:
  un - **un**happy   il - **il**legal   in - **in**active
  non - **non**washable im - **im**mature

Write an appropriate prefix:

3. A. _____ stop   C. _____ decisive   E. _____ possible
   B. _____ legible   D. _____ kind

PARTS OF SPEECH: PRONOUNS

A pronoun takes the place of a noun.
    Examples: girl - **she** or **her**   boy - **he** or **him**   car - **it**

Write a pronoun in each blank:

4. Carlo and _____ pulled out stools and sat on _____.

ANALOGIES:

Circle the correct answer:

5. tell : ask :: defend : _____
   (a) protect   (b) championship   (c) guard   (d) attack

SENTENCE COMBINING:

6. Jasmin made a dress.
   The dress is pink.
   The dress is flowered.

DAY 13

CAPITALIZATION:

1. for christmas dinner, her mother served new england clam chowder.

PUNCTUATION:

2. Yikes Youre here already

PARTS OF SPEECH: CONJUNCTIONS
Conjunctions are joining words. The three most commonly used conjunctions are *and*, *but*, and *or*. These are called coordinating conjunctions.

Write two appropriate conjunctions:

3. A. Jack _____ his dad will be shopping for groceries.
   B. Jack _____ his dad will be shopping for groceries.

PARTS OF SPEECH: VERBS
<u>May</u> is used to ask permission or to express that someone or something could possibly do something.
  Examples: *May* I go, too?   I *may* go to Canada this summer.
<u>Can</u> means *to be able.*   Example: Mary *can* build sturdy birdhouses.

Circle the correct verb:

4. A. (May, Can) we sleep in a tent on our next camping trip?
   B. (May, Can) you break this in two for me?

SPELLING:

Write the correct spelling of these words:

5. A. vote + ing - _____
   B. pale + ness - _____

SENTENCE COMBINING:

6. Quahana Parker was a great Comanche chief.
   Micah is related to him.

_____

_____

DAY 14

CAPITALIZATION:

1. the first u. s. government was formed under the articles of confederation.

PUNCTUATION:
   Write the abbreviation:

2. A. mountain - _____   B. inch - _____   C. avenue - _____

PARTS OF SPEECH: PREPOSITIONS
   Prepositional phrases begin with a preposition and end with a noun or a pronoun (such as *me, him, her, us,* or *them*). Commonly used prepositions are *to, for, from, in, into, on,* and *with.*

   Circle any prepositional phrases:

3. This note from Mr. Davis is for my mom.

PARTS OF SPEECH: VERBS
   Circle the correct verb:

4. Their mother has (went, gone) to the airport.

ANALOGIES:
   Circle the correct answer:

5. weak : strong :: build : _____
   (a) destroy   (b) contractor   (c) erect   (d) blueprints

SENTENCE COMBINING:

6. The spine protects the spinal cord.
   The spine also forms the backbone of the skeleton.

_____

_____

DAY 15

CAPITALIZATION:

1. dear clint,

    dr. vendi, our veterinarian, came to examine our new horse last saturday.

                                                    always,

                                                    lulu

PUNCTUATION:

2. Were staying until 5 30 P M on Sunday April 1

PARTS OF SPEECH: ADVERBS
  Circle the correct adverb:

3. Holly runs (faster, fastest) than her sister.

PARTS OF SPEECH: VERBS
   There are twenty-three helping (auxiliary) verbs.
  Unscramble these nine helping verbs:

4. A. dosluh - _____ D. lshal - _____ G. eb - _____

   B. dowlu - _____ E. liwl - _____ H. gebin - _____

   C. doclu - _____ F. nac - _____ I. nebe - _____

SPELLING:

  Write the correct spelling of these words:

5. A. blaze + ed - _____

   B. rehearse + ing - _____

   C. trump + et - _____

SENTENCE COMBINING:

6. A rattlesnake has a forked tongue.
   It is a venomous snake.

_____

_____

DAY 16

CAPITALIZATION:
   Capitalize a proper adjective but not the noun it modifies.
   Example: Portugal (noun)   -   Portuguese (proper adjective)
           He worked for a **P**ortuguese boat captain for two years.

1. did betsy ross make the first american flag in boston?

PUNCTUATION:
   Use underlining or quotation marks:

2. A. Homeward to America   (title of a book)   B. Dexter McDwyer   (title of a poem)

PREFIXES/ROOTS/SUFFIXES:
   A root is a base from which words are formed. Some roots can stand alone as a word; some form only a part of a word.
   ***Therm* is a root that relates to heat.**
   Using this information, explain the word, *thermometer*:

3. _____

PARTS OF SPEECH: NOUNS
   Circle any nouns:

4. His brother just bought a van.

SPELLING:
   A word ending with vowel + vowel + consonant (VVC) usually just adds a suffix.   Examples: reap + ed = reap**ed**   bait + ing = bait**ing**
   Write the correct spelling of these words:

5. A. braid + ed - _____   C. boil + ing - _____
   B. steam + er - _____   D. tear + ful - _____

SENTENCE COMBINING:

6. Plants use sunlight to make their food.
   Plants use water to make their food.
   Plants use carbon dioxide to make their food.

   _____

   _____

DAY 17

CAPITALIZATION:

1. we read about africa's victoria falls last march.

PUNCTUATION:

2. Marta muttered   Your feet are covered with mud

PARTS OF SPEECH: VERBS
   Some verbs can serve as either a helping verb or a main verb.
   A main verb stands alone.
      Example: Jemima <u>does</u> her homework at four o'clock.
   A verb phrase consists of helping verb(s) plus a main verb.
      Example: Jemima <u>does</u> not <u>like</u> science very much.
   Place a √ if the sentence contains a helping verb:

3. A. ___ Carlos <u>did</u> the dishes.   C. ___ I <u>have</u> an old penny.
   B. ___ We <u>did</u> not <u>want</u> advice.   D. ___ <u>Do</u> you <u>have</u> a plastic funnel?

PARTS OF SPEECH: NOUNS
   Plural means more than one.
   Most plurals are formed by adding s to the noun.
   Place a √ if the plural is formed by adding s.

4. A. ___ fist   B. ___ request   C. ___ cry   D. ___ hunch

SPELLING:
   One-syllable words ending in consonant + vowel + consonant (CVC) usually double the final consonant when adding a suffix beginning with a VOWEL. They usually do not change when adding a suffix beginning with a consonant. Examples: trim + ing = trimming   trim + ness = trimness
   Write the correct spelling of these words:

5. A.   clap + ed - _____   B.   drab + ness - _____

SENTENCE COMBINING:

6. The circus is coming to town.
   I cannot attend.

DAY 18

CAPITALIZATION:

1. last summer, dr. and mrs. j. r. stone went to everglades national park in florida.

PUNCTUATION:

2. Was the two oclock bus Ms Dunfy on time today

PARTS OF SPEECH: VERBS
Circle the correct verb:

3. Please (sit, set) beside me.

WORDS:
Circle the correct word:

4. They took their dog on an outing, (too, to, two).

ANALOGIES:
Circle the correct answer:

5. car : automobile :: color : _____
   (a) rainbow   (b) crayon   (c) hue   (d) colorless

SENTENCE COMBINING:

6. Hang gliders use currents of hot, rising air to stay aloft.
   These hot, rising air currents are called thermals.

_____

_____

DAY 19

CAPITALIZATION:

1. did walter cronkite, a famous journalist, work for colonial broadcasting system?

PUNCTUATION:

2. Susan did Mrs Prince arrive for her appointment at 2 30

PARTS OF SPEECH: VERBS
   Circle the correct verb:

3. Have you (chose, chosen) the most colorful frame?

PHRASES/CLAUSES:
   A phrase is a group of words.   Example: with my aunt
   A clause contains a subject and a verb.
      Example: While I was eating
   Write P if the words form a phrase; write C if the words form a clause:

4. A. _____ For five minutes   B. _____ When Bo laughs

ANALOGIES:
   The first word of an analogy may express a general topic, and the second word may state a type/category of that topic. Choose the answer that has the same relationship to the third word.
      Example: Book : mystery :: tree : _____
         (a) woods   (b) hiking   **(c) oak**   (d) winter
   Circle the correct answer:

5. meal : breakfast :: gem : _____
   (a) ruby   (b) precious   (c) jewelry   (d) metal

SENTENCE COMBINING:

6. A solid is a type of matter.
   A liquid is a type of matter.
   A gas is a type of matter.

_____

_____

DAY 20

CAPITALIZATION:

1. on april fools' day, mayor dougal usually goes to the bahama islands.

PUNCTUATION:
   Place a comma between two adjectives that describe unless one adjective is a color or a number.
   Examples: *Bright, shiny* shells were strung on a bracelet.
   *Twinkling **red*** lights shone in the dark.

2. Long sharp hooks stuck out from Miras fishing lure

PARTS OF SPEECH: ADJECTIVES/ADVERBS
   Good **is a describing word (adjective).**   Example: They are good artists.
   Well **is an adverb that tells *how*.**   Example: They draw well.
   Circle the correct word:

3. Kimo is a (good, well) baker; he makes crescent rolls especially (good, well).

PREFIXES/ROOTS/SUFFIXES:
   A root is a base from which words are formed. Some roots can stand alone as a word; some form only a part of a word.
   ***Vis* is a root that has to do with sight.**
   Using this information, explain the word, *vision*:

4. _____

ANALOGIES:
   Circle the correct answer:

5. chair : rocker :: boat : _____
   (a) lake   (b) oar   (c) canoe   (d) banks

SENTENCE COMBINING:

6. Ben will give his sister a necklace.
   The necklace is gold.
   The necklace has three pearls.

   _____

   _____

DAY 21

CAPITALIZATION:

1. the aztec indians of mexico were conquered by cortez.

PUNCTUATION:

2. No his name wasnt listed as Romero Roberto

PARTS OF SPEECH: PREPOSITIONS
   A prepositional phrase is a group of words that begins with a preposition. The object of the preposition (O.P.) is the word (noun or pronoun) that ends a prepositional phrase.
   Example: Lolita ran **to her room**.   *Room* is the object of the preposition.
Circle the prepositional phrase; label the object of the preposition - O.P.:

3. The children were playing in the rain.

PARTS OF SPEECH: NOUNS
   A possessive noun shows ownership.
   If the noun is singular (one), place an apostrophe (') + s to form the possessive.   Example: boots belonging to Todd: Todd's boots

4. A. a truck belonging to Pat - _____
    B. a mayor of that town - _____

SPELLING:
   Write the correct spelling of these words:

5. A. bowl + er - _____
    B. thin + ed - _____
    C. sense + less - _____

SENTENCE COMBINING:

6. Supersonic jets can travel faster than the speed of sound.
    This is called Mach 1.

_____

_____

DAY 22

CAPITALIZATION:

1. the marzanno family owns an italian restaurant called roma gardens.

PUNCTUATION:
An interrupter is a word or group of words that can be used for emphasis. Example: These apples are, **in fact,** rotten.
An interrupter can add an additional thought.
Example: This orange, **I think,** was grown in Florida.
Use commas to set off interrupters.

2. The weather I believe will be clear today

SYNONYMS/ANTONYMS/HOMONYMS:
Homonyms are words that sound alike but are spelled differently.
Synonyms are words with similar meanings.

3. A. Write a homonym for flea: _____
   B. Write a synonym for tug: _____

SUBJECT/VERB:
A compound subject means that there are *two or more* subjects.
Example: My <u>cousin</u> and <u>I</u> play two-square.
Underline the subject once and the verb twice:

4. Her jacket and mittens match.

ANALOGIES:
Circle the correct answer:

5. candy : fudge :: sport : _____
   (a) ball   (b) stadium   (c) athlete   (d) tennis

SENTENCE COMBINING:

6. Jamilla takes acting lessons.
   She wants to become a Broadway actress.

_____

_____

DAY 23

CAPITALIZATION:

1. a french pilot, louis bleriot, crossed the english channel in a monoplane.

PUNCTUATION:

2. Stop the car   exclaimed Chan

PARTS OF SPEECH: ADVERBS
   Use *well* to describe how someone is doing (has done) something.
   Circle the correct word:
3. The baby took his first step last week and is now walking (good, well).

PARTS OF SPEECH: INTERJECTIONS
   Circle the interjection:
4. Yikes! I nearly lost my balance and fell off the balance beam!

SPELLING:
Remember:
   Words ending VVC do not usually change when adding any suffix.
      Example: load + ed = loaded
   Words ending VCC do not usually change when adding any suffix.
      Example: bend + ing = bending
   Words ending consonant + e usually drop the e when adding a suffix that begins with a vowel. They usually do not drop the e when adding a suffix that begins with a consonant. Example: hope + ful = hopeful
   Write the correct spelling of these words:

5. A. love + ly - _____
   B. press + ure - _____
   C. tour + ing - _____

SENTENCE COMBINING:

6. The platypus is a mammal.
   It lays eggs.

DAY 24

CAPITALIZATION:

1. last summer, grandpa raced stock cars at paradise speedway in alabama.

PUNCTUATION:

2.
                                (A)   16329 Blackmore Lane
                                                    Henderson NV 89015
                                                    June 20 20--

    (B)   Dear Miss Sells

FRIENDLY LETTER:
    There are five parts to a friendly letter: heading, closing, signature, salutation (greeting), and body.

    Use the letter in #2 to answer these questions:

3. A. Part A is the: 1) body   2) salutation   3) heading   4) closing
   B. Part B is the: 1) closing 2) salutation   3) signature   4) body

SENTENCE TYPES:
    An imperative sentence gives a command. It expresses a complete thought and ends with a period.

    Place a √ if the sentence is imperative:

4. A. ___ Raise your right hand.
   B. ___ Tate raised his right hand.
   C. ___ Raise your right hand, please.

ANALOGIES:
Circle the correct answer:

5. save : spend :: collect : _____
   (a) tax   (b) distribute   (c) require   (d) cower

SENTENCE COMBINING:

6. The twenty teeth a baby first gets are called primary teeth.
   They are also called milk teeth.

_____

_____

DAY 25

CAPITALIZATION:

1. pisgah national park is in the blue ridge mountains of north carolina.

PUNCTUATION:

2. Bruce Rick and Nathan went to the Y M C A to exercise

SUBJECT/VERB:
The subject of a sentence tells *who* or *what* the sentence is about.
The verb tells what *is (was)* or what *happens (happened)*.

Note: Prepositional phrases usually aren't subject or verb. Deleting them makes finding the subject and verb easier.
Example: <u>Janell</u> <u>ran</u> with her brother.

Underline the subject once and the verb or verb phrase twice:

3. During the summer, Logan worked at a dude ranch.

PARTS OF SPEECH: NOUNS
Plural means more than one.
Words ending in *s, sh, ch, x,* and *z* add <u>es</u> to form the plural.

4. A. A word that ends in *sh* is _____; its plural is _____.
   B. A word that ends in *x* is _____; its plural is _____.
   C. A word that ends in *s* is _____; its plural is _____.

ANALOGIES:

Circle the correct answer:

5. migrate : move :: moisten : _____
   (a) dampen   (b) moisture   (c) dried   (d) fasten

SENTENCE COMBINING:

6. Kami's mother is an author.
   She writes children's books.

DAY 26

CAPITALIZATION:

1. william l. shoemaker, a successful jockey, won four kentucky derbies.

PUNCTUATION:

2. Outing List
    -bandages
    -bottled water
    -toothbrush

PARTS OF SPEECH: VERBS
  Some verbs can serve as either a helping verb or a main verb.
    Example: Garth **had** a cavity.   (main verb)
  A verb phrase consists of helping verb(s) plus a main verb.
    Example: Garth **had gone** to his dentist.   (helping verb)
  Place a √ if the sentence contains a helping verb:

3. A. ___ Faith <u>has</u> a rash on her hand.   C. ___ The soup <u>is</u> <u>simmering</u>.
   B. ___ Our mirror <u>has</u> <u>cracked</u> again.   D. ___ Kim <u>is</u> two years old.

PARTS OF SPEECH: ADVERBS
  Circle any adverbs that tell *where:*

4. The banker set her papers aside and looked up.

SPELLING:
  Write the correct spelling of these words:

5. A. scare + ed - _____
   B. fresh + ly - _____
   C. repair + ing - _____

SENTENCE COMBINING:

6. Her brother joined the U. S. Marine Corps.
   He is stationed at Camp Pendleton.

   _____

   _____

DAY 27

CAPITALIZATION:

1. the band from daltson high school marched at a columbus day parade.

PUNCTUATION:

2. The Rev D G Raineri visited patients at St Marys Hospital at 6 P M

PARTS OF SPEECH: VERBS

The present tense tells what *is* or what *is happening* now.
   Example: Bill <u>collects</u> marbles.

The past tense tells <u>past time</u>.
   Example: Someone <u>collected</u> the papers.

Write <u>PR</u> if the tense is present; write <u>PT</u> if the tense is past:

3. _____ The child and her father <u>blew</u> bubbles from a jar.

PARTS OF SPEECH: ADJECTIVES

Write a describing adjective; draw an arrow to the noun it describes:

4. Many _____ rugs were on the _____ floor.

SPELLING:

Write the correct spelling of these words:

5. A. fashion + able - _____

   B. release + ing - _____

   C. press + ed - _____

SENTENCE COMBINING:

6. A butterwort is a plant.
   It traps insects with the sap on its leaves.

   _____

   _____

DAY 28

CAPITALIZATION:

1. on thanksgiving, miss bengall and i ate at cobbler's inn.

PUNCTUATION:

2. The pilot studied her flight plan checked her watch and boarded the plane

PARTS OF SPEECH: PRONOUNS

A pronoun takes the place of a noun.
I, he, she, we, they, you, and *it* can serve as the subject of a sentence.

Write a pronoun in each blank:

3. My friend and _____ like math; _____ really enjoy(s) measuring angles.

PARTS OF SPEECH: ADJECTIVES

Circle the correct adjective:

4. My left shoe seems (tighter, tightest) than my right one.

ANALOGIES:

Circle the correct answer:

5. forgiving : unforgiving :: lazy : _____
 (a) idle   (b) lazier   (c) industrious   (d) sluggish

SENTENCE COMBINING:

6. Pia lives on Rainbow Avenue.
 She lives in an apartment complex.
 Tim lives in the same apartments.

_____

_____

DAY 29

CAPITALIZATION:
Capitalize these titles:

1. A. <u>sequoia scout</u>　　B. <u>cannons of the comstock</u>　　C. <u>the key to zion</u>

PUNCTUATION:

2. Their business address is 2193 Cold Creek Drive Sandpoint ID 83864

PREFIXES/ROOTS/SUFFIXES:

Prefixes help to understand word meaning. Some prefixes are used to express numbers.
　　uni, mono - 1 (unicycle); (monorail)
　　bi, du - 2 (bilateral); (dual)
　　tri - 3 (tricity)

Write an appropriate prefix:

3. A. Yancy's new _____cycle has two huge red wheels.
   B. The toddler rode a three-wheeled vehicle, a _____cycle.
   C. The _____cycle, a one-wheeled vehicle, was hard for me to ride.
   D. When only one person speaks, it is called a _____logue.

PARTS OF SPEECH:　　NOUNS

Write C if the noun is common; write P if the noun is proper:

Remember: A *type* of a person, place, or thing is still a common noun.

4. A. ____ DAY　　　B. ____ FRIDAY　　　C. ____ HOLIDAY

ANALOGIES:
Circle the correct answer:

5. bear : polar :: bridge : _____
   (a) building　　(b) suspension　　(c) water　　(d) ship

SENTENCE COMBINING:

6. Robins live in a nest.
   The nest is located at the top of that maple tree.

_____

_____

DAY 30

CAPITALIZATION:

1. her uncle from canada speaks english and french.

PUNCTUATION:
   Use underlining or quotation marks:

2. A. Air Bud   (title of a movie)
   B. It's Feeding Time   (title of a newspaper article)

PARTS OF SPEECH: VERBS
   The present tense tells what *is* or what *is happening* now.
   The past tense tells *what has already happened*.

   Write PR if the tense is present; write PT if the tense is past:

3. A. _____ Marco <u>goes</u> to nearly every art show.
   B. _____ Paula <u>delivered</u> several boxes to her mother's office.

PARTS OF SPEECH: PRONOUNS
   Circle the correct usage:

4. (Me and my friend, My friend and I, My friend and me) are ready to help.

ANALOGIES:
   Circle the correct answer:

5. parsley : herb :: manatee : _____
   (a) mammal   (b) dolphin   (c) otter   (d) ocean

SENTENCE COMBINING:

6. A small galaxy may contain about 100,000 stars.
   A large galaxy may contain 3,000 billion stars.

   _____

   _____

DAY 31

CAPITALIZATION:

1. at cost club, i was given a coupon for parchy* crackers.

*brand name

PUNCTUATION:

2. Dear Alicia
   My family and I left for Mexico City on Friday January 19 2001
                                                        Love
                                                        Toni

PARTS OF SPEECH: ADVERBS
   Circle any adverbs that tell *how or when*:

3. They often watch the news together.

PARTS OF SPEECH: NOUNS
   Some nouns do not change when forming the plural.   sheep - sheep

4. An example of a noun that does not change is _____.

ANALOGIES:
   Analogies may have a relationship of *part to whole*.
   Finger : hand :: handle : _____
   (a) wagon   (b) knob   (c) open   (d) lever

   Finger is part of a hand. The third word is *handle*. *Handle* must be a part of an item. Therefore, the answer is *wagon*. A *handle* is part of a *wagon*.

   Circle the correct answer:

5. hoof : horse :: claw : _____
   (a) cat   (b) talon   (c) sharp   (d) animal

SENTENCE COMBINING:

6. Each body cell has fluid material.
   This fluid material is called cytoplasm.

_____

_____

DAY 32

CAPITALIZATION:

1. did aunt susan attend a community meeting held at friendship bible church?

PUNCTUATION:

2. The boys bathroom is locked   said Jacy

PARTS OF SPEECH: VERBS
Write the contraction:

3. A. he is - _____   D. you are - _____
   B. we will - _____   E. they have - _____
   C. were not - _____   F. I shall - _____

SENTENCES/FRAGMENTS/RUN-ONS:

Write S if the words form a sentence; write F for fragment if the words do not form a sentence:

4. A. _____ Many in the middle of the afternoon.
   B. _____ Many campers set up tents in the middle of the afternoon.

ANALOGIES:
Circle the correct answer:

5. heel : foot :: sole : _____
   (a) soul   (b) shoe   (c) toe   (d) leg

SENTENCE COMBINING:

6. The cupboard is pine.
   The cupboard is three-cornered.
   The cupboard has glass doors.

   _____

   _____

DAY 33

CAPITALIZATION:

1. many pioneers crossed the mississippi river at st. louis, missouri.

PUNCTUATION:

2. Gov Thon and her husband visited Hartford Connecticut

PARTS OF SPEECH: VERBS
   A regular verb adds ed to the past and past participle.
                            past   **past participle**
   Example: to wave   **waved**   (had) wav**ed**

   An irregular verb changes to form the past and past participle.
   Example: to sing   **sang**   (had) **sung**

   Place a √ if the verb is regular:

3. A. ___ to lean   C. ___ to praise   E. ___ to swim
   B. ___ to fly   D. ___ to rise   F. ___ to make

DICTIONARY SKILLS: ALPHABETIZING
   Alphabetize these words:

4. grab   core   great   easy   heart   crime

ANALOGIES:

   Circle the correct answer:

5. sleeve : coat :: anchor : _____
   (a) ship   (b) metal   (c) weight   (d) movement

SENTENCE COMBINING:

6. Her favorite food is chicken.
   She likes it marinated in mustard sauce.

_____

_____

DAY 34

CAPITALIZATION:

1. jay is attending the schooner days and blues festival in rockland, maine.

PUNCTUATION:

2. No I dont want milk juice or soda

PARTS OF SPEECH: PREPOSITIONS
A prepositional phrase is a group of words that begins with a preposition. The object of the preposition is the word (noun or pronoun) that ends a prepositional phrase.
       Examples: from his **mother**   with **us**
Circle the prepositional phrase; label the object of the preposition - <u>O.P.</u>:

3. This gift is for Lani.

PARTS OF SPEECH: NOUNS
   A concrete noun names a real thing.
   An abstract noun names an idea.

Write <u>C</u> if the noun is concrete; write <u>A</u> if the noun is abstract:

4. A. _____ faith   B. _____ protection   C. _____ fort

ANALOGIES:

 Circle the correct answer:

5. act : play :: stanza : _____
   (a) meter   (b) lines   (c) story   (d) poem

SENTENCE COMBINING:

6. Maria hit the softball.
   Maria ran to first base.
   Maria waved her hands excitedly.

_____

_____

DAY 35

CAPITALIZATION:

1. lida yelled, "don't touch that south african mamba!"

PUNCTUATION:

2. Toby do I add one half cup of cream to this dessert

SENTENCE TYPES:
An exclamatory sentence shows excitement or some other strong emotion. It expresses a complete thought and ends with an exclamation point.

Place a √ if the sentence is exclamatory:

3. A. ___ I can do it!
   B. ___ Yikes! I left my money in the bathroom!
   C. ___ She is a terrific hockey player.

PARTS OF SPEECH: ADVERBS
Circle the correct adverb:

4. She pressed (harder, hardest) on the third lever.

ANALOGIES:
The first two words of an analogy may express whole to part. Then, the answer must express a part of the third item.

    Example: watermelon : slice :: boot : _____
        (a) shoe   **(b) heel**   (c) leather   (d) work

Circle the correct answer:

5. team : player :: herd : _____
   (a) ranch   (b) round-up   (c) steer   (d) clan

SENTENCE COMBINING:

6. This oven cleaner is effective.
   This cleaner is poisonous.

_____

_____

DAY 36

CAPITALIZATION:

1. dear nikko,
    i'll be leaving in the morning. thanks for everything.
                                  your friend,
                                  ricky

PUNCTUATION:

2. Well whos the companys new vice president

SUBJECT/VERB:
Compound means more than one.
Underline the compound subject once and the verb or verb phrase twice:

3. Scissors and tape fell from her hands.

PARTS OF SPEECH: ADJECTIVES/ADVERBS
Write *good* or *well*:

4. This is a _____ story; you write _____.

ANALOGIES:
Circle the correct answer:

5. shoe : foot :: glove : _____
   (a) hand   (b) mitten   (c) winter   (d) clothing

SENTENCE COMBINING:

6. It has rained for two days.
   Edroe Street is flooded.

   _____

   _____

DAY 37

CAPITALIZATION:

1. the qin dynasty in china reigned from 255-206 b. c.

PUNCTUATION:
   Punctuate this outline:

2. I   Flowers
      A   Bulbs
         1   Daffodils
         2   Tulips
      B   Seedlings
   II   Shrubs

PARTS OF SPEECH: ADVERBS/ADJECTIVES
   Circle the correct word:

3. Ellie kicked that ball (good, well).

SUBJECT/VERB:
   A compound verb means that there are *two or more* verbs.
   Underline the subject once and the verb twice:

4. Shannon raised her hand and waved.

SPELLING:
   A one-syllable word ending with consonant + vowel + consonant (CVC) will usually double the final consonant when adding a suffix beginning with a VOWEL. It will not double the final consonant when adding a suffix beginning with a consonant.
      Examples: ship + ing = shipping   ship + ment = shipment
   Write the correct spelling of these words:

5. A. beg + ing - _____   C. scar + ed - _____

   B. but + er - _____   D. cap + tion - _____

SENTENCE COMBINING:

6. Luke bought groceries.
   Before that, he went to the bank.

_____

_____

DAY 38

CAPITALIZATION:

1. does st. basil's cathedral in russia have an onion-shaped dome?

PUNCTUATION:

2. Pictures of a writers conference appeared in a two page layout

PREFIXES/ROOTS/SUFFIXES:

    A suffix is an ending; it is added to a root.
        Ward or wards are suffixes that mean *in a given direction.*
    Using this information, explain the word, *westward:*

3. _____

SUBJECT/VERB:

    Underline the subject; circle the verb that agrees with the subject:

4. After the ice storm, the roads (was, were) very dangerous.

SPELLING:

    Write the correct spelling of these words:

5. A. insure + ance - _____

   B. drop + ed - _____

   C. trust + ing - _____

SENTENCE COMBINING:

6. These pants need to be ironed.
These pants are wrinkled.

_____

_____

DAY 39

CAPITALIZATION:

1. in history class, molly and ryan studied about the incas of peru.

PUNCTUATION:

An appositive is a noun or noun phrase (more than one word) that is placed beside another noun to explain it. Use commas before and after an appositive.

Example: Mt. Fuji, **a mountain in Japan,** is beautiful.

2. Sparky our new dog is our familys first pet

PARTS OF SPEECH: NOUNS
Circle any nouns:

3. Bob and his sister went to a beach in Texas.

PARTS OF SPEECH: VERBS
Circle the correct verb:

4. A. They had (rode, ridden) their horses into a canyon.
   B. Her aunt must have (flown, flew) to Wyoming on business.
   C. That contractor should have (builded, built) his house closer to the road.

ANALOGIES:
Circle the correct answer:

5. flashy : showy :: fidgety : _____
   (a) sensitive   (b) inactive   (c) hibernate   (d) restless

SENTENCE COMBINING:

6. Jana's watercolor won a prize.
   It was of a parrot.
   She was very happy.

_____

_____

DAY 40

CAPITALIZATION:

1. the himalaya mountains in asia extend for thousands of miles.

PUNCTUATION:
   Write the abbreviation:

2. A. building - _____   B. pint - _____   C. teaspoon - _____

PREFIXES/ROOTS/SUFFIXES:
   A root is a base from which words are formed.
   Script is a root that relates to writing.
   Using this information, explain the word, *inscription*:

3. _____

PARTS OF SPEECH: ADJECTIVES/ADVERBS
   Good is a describing word (adjective).   Example: They are good artists.
   Well is an adverb that tells how.   Example: They draw well.
   When stating a person's health, use *well*.   Example: I don't feel well.
   Circle the correct word:

4. A. Lars is a (good, well) plumber.
    B. After having a tetanus shot, Penny didn't feel (good, well).

ANALOGIES:
   Circle the correct answer:

5. captured : released :: common : _____
    (a) normal   (b) extraordinary   (c) plain   (d) familiar

SENTENCE COMBINING:

6. The world's largest desert is the Sahara.
    It covers nearly one-third of Africa.

    _____

    _____

DAY 41

CAPITALIZATION:
Capitalize this outline:
1. i. clocks
    a. mainspring
    b. pendulum
   ii. watches

PUNCTUATION:

2. Hes twenty one and a diver from Bangor Maine

PARTS OF SPEECH: VERBS
Circle the correct verb:

3. You (may, can) go with us if you want.

WORDS:
Their shows ownership.   Example: *Their* cat is a Persian.
There shows place.   Example: Go *there* in the morning.
They're is a contraction for they are.   Example: *They're* next in line.
Circle the correct word:

4. A. He sat (there, they're, their) in silence.
   B. (There, They're, Their) planning a surprise for (there, they're, their) sister.

ANALOGIES:
Circle the correct answer:

5. cards : birthday :: games : _____
   (a) activities   (b) fun   (c) board   (d) events

SENTENCE COMBINING:

6. James Naismith created the game of basketball.
   He did this for the Y. M. C. A.
   The year was 1891.

_____

_____

DAY 42

CAPITALIZATION:

1. the battle of yorktown ended the american revolution.

PUNCTUATION:

2. Kenny asked Wheres my red baseball cap

PARTS OF SPEECH: CONJUNCTIONS
Circle any coordinating conjunctions:

3. Dakota and his brother will attend the play, but they'll buy tickets at the door.

FRIENDLY LETTERS/ENVELOPES:

4. _____

   Tara Hill
   222 North 81st Street
   Scottsdale, AZ   85267

                                Noah Liston
                                4937 East Oak Street
                                Gettysburg, PA   17325

   _____

   A. Who is sending this letter? _____
   B. What is on the third line of the return address? _____

ANALOGIES:
Circle the correct answer:

5. movement : motion :: scent : _____
   (a) aroma   (b) scenic   (c) delivered   (d) flowers

SENTENCE COMBINING:

6. The boy emailed his friends.
   The boy then went to meet his friends.

   _____

   _____

DAY 43

CAPITALIZATION:

1. susan asked, "did a british man build a steam locomotive called the <u>rocket</u>?"

PUNCTUATION:

An interrupter is a word or group of words that can be used for emphasis. Example: His dad**, obviously,** likes to sail.

An interrupter can add an additional thought.
Example: My aunt**, as a matter of fact,** owns this restaurant.
Use commas to set off interrupters.

2. This beef jerky without a doubt is the toughest Ive ever eaten

PARTS OF SPEECH: PRONOUNS
A pronoun takes the place of a noun.
Me, him, her, us, them, you, and *it* can serve as an object of a sentence.

Write an appropriate pronoun:

3. The coach told Mona and _____ to go into the game.

WORDS:

Circle the correct word:

4. A. (Their, There, They're) ad has not appeared in the newspaper.
   B. Would you like to travel (there, their, they're)?
   C. They want (too, to, two) pack early.
   D. (May, Can) you lift this bucket of water?

ANALOGIES:

Circle the correct answer:

5. empty : vacant :: pretty : _____
   (a) beckoning   (b) attractive   (c) entering   (d) hollow

SENTENCE COMBINING:

6. His aunt is visiting from Detroit.
   She is only staying for two days.

_____

_____

DAY 44

CAPITALIZATION:

1. my uncle darius lives near the savannah river in the south.

PUNCTUATION:

2. Dear Mr and Mrs Bencze **(A)**
    Yes youre invited to visit us in Santiago Chile **(B)**
        Respectfully **(C)**
        Ria **(D)**

FRIENDLY LETTER:
   There are five parts to a friendly letter: heading, closing, signature, greeting (salutation), and body.
   Write the parts of the letter shown in #2:

3. A. _____   C. _____
   B. _____   D. _____

PARTS OF SPEECH: NOUNS
   Write the plural ending:

4. A. wax____   B. prong____   C. lens____   D. rich____

ANALOGIES:
   Some analogies show the relationship of an item and its use.
   Choose an answer that has the same relationship to the third word.
        Example: iron : press :: toothbrush : _____
                   (a) teeth   **(b) clean**   (c) sleep   (d) gums
   Circle the correct answer:

5. saw : cut :: ladle : _____
   (a) pierce   (b) scoop   (c) spread   (d) fork

SENTENCE COMBINING:

6. Lake Baikal is in Russia.
   It is the world's largest freshwater lake.

_____

_____

DAY 45

CAPITALIZATION:

1. did dad study the chinese language at a college in the east?

PUNCTUATION:

2. Sasha lifted her long well toned arm to shoot the basketball

SENTENCES/FRAGMENTS/RUN-ONS:

Write *S* if the words form a sentence; write *F* for fragment if the words do not form a sentence:

3. A. _____ Hal hit the nail squarely on the head.
   B. _____ During the afternoon, roamed through the woods.

SUBJECT/VERB:

Underline the subject once and the verb or verb phrase twice:

4. The rabbi and his son visited a homeless shelter.

ANALOGIES:

Circle the correct answer:

5. mixer : combine :: lasso : _____
   (a) chase   (b) rodeo   (c) hemp   (d) catch

SENTENCE COMBINING:

6. These pears are juicy.
   These pears are ripe.
   These pears are large.

_____

_____

DAY 46

CAPITALIZATION:

1. during the middle ages, castles were built in england.

PUNCTUATION:

2. Whoa This ski lift is so high exclaimed Miss Dee

SUBJECT/VERB:
Underline the subject once and the verb or verb phrase twice:

3. Their suitcases toppled from the conveyor belt at the airport.

DICTIONARY SKILLS: GUIDE WORDS

Two words appear in boldfaced type at the top of each dictionary page. These are called guide words. The first word listed is the first word (entry) on that page. The second word listed is the last word (entry) on that page.
    Example: dangerous - dim

Place a √ if the word will appear on a page with the guide words:
    badge - beside:

4. A. ___ band   B. ___ brain   C. ___ back   D. ___ berth

ANALOGIES:
Circle the correct answer:

5. limousine : transport :: umbrella : _____
   (a) rain   (b) carry   (c) protect   (d) flourish

SENTENCE COMBINING:

6. Mr. Hart became perturbed.
   Mr. Hart received another incorrect bill.

_____

_____

DAY 47

CAPITALIZATION:

1. his aunt belongs to the frequent traveler club sponsored by atlantic airlines.

PUNCTUATION:

2. Lena said   My uncle lives in Naco Mexico

SYNONYMS/ANTONYMS/HOMONYMS:
   Homonyms are words that sound alike but are spelled differently.
   Synonyms are words that have similar meanings.
   Antonyms are words with opposite meanings.

   Write **H** if the words are homonyms, **S** if the words are synonyms, and **A** if the words are antonyms:

3. A. ___ love - detest   B. ___ doctor - physican   C. ___ gait - gate

PARTS OF SPEECH: NOUNS
   A common noun does not name a specific person, place, or thing.
   A proper noun names a specific person, place, or thing.
      A *type* is a common noun.

4. A. Write a common noun: _____
    B. Write a proper noun: _____

ANALOGIES:

   Circle the correct answer:

5. peeler : pare :: yardstick : _____
    (a) ruler   (b) measure   (c) distance   (d) feet

SENTENCE COMBINING:

6. The raft is square.
    The raft is large.
    It is slightly deflated.

_____

_____

DAY 48

CAPITALIZATION:

1. a hispanic festival was held near fairmont parkway last friday.

PUNCTUATION:
Place commas before and after a title that follows a name within a sentence. Example: Mona Hu, D.O., is their physician.

2. Sal Rice R N works at St Johns Hospital in Jackson Mississippi

PREFIXES/ROOTS/SUFFIXES:
The prefixes, *pre* and *fore*, are commonly used to express *before*:
    pre - **pre**plan   fore - **fore**tell

Write an appropriate prefix:

3. A. ____heat   B. ____wash   C. ____warn   D. ____told

PHRASES/CLAUSES:
A phrase is a group of words. Example: beyond that goal post
A clause contains a subject and a verb. Example: When <u>you</u> <u>smile</u>
Write P if the words form a phrase; write C if the words form a clause:

4. A. _____ Except a few shrimpers   B. _____ After we wrote our stories

ANALOGIES:
Sometimes, the first two words will be nouns but still reflect "used by."
    Example: Bow : archer :: vase : _____
    (a) flowers (b) urn (c) water **(d) florist**
A *bow* is used by an *archer*; a *vase* is used by a *florist*.

Circle the correct answer:

5. clay : potter :: wood : _____
   (a) tree (b) forest (c) carver (d) mayor

SENTENCE COMBINING:

6. The monkey is swinging.
   The monkey is making funny faces.

_____

_____

DAY 49

CAPITALIZATION:

1. has mayor miller spoken at the rotary club?

PUNCTUATION:

2. Jay asked   Whos Lisas teacher

PARTS OF SPEECH: ADJECTIVES

When a linking verb such as *to taste, to smell,* **or** *to look* **is used in a sentence and** *was or were* **can replace it, use** good, **not** *well.*

                                               were
Example: The seaweed cookies <u>tasted</u> good.

Replace the linking verb with *was* **or** *were*; **circle the correct word:**

3. The freshly baked bread smelled (good, well).

PREFIXES/ROOTS/SUFFIXES:

A suffix is an ending; it is added to a root.
   Ly is a suffix that can mean *happening again at specific times.*

Using this information, explain the word, *weekly.*

4. _____

SPELLING:

Write the correct spelling of these words:

5. A.   map + ing - _____
    B.   relish + ed - _____
    C.   refine + ment - _____

SENTENCE COMBINING:

6. We planted daisies in our flower garden.
   We planted petunias in our flower garden.
   We planted daffodils in our flower garden.

_____

_____

DAY 50

CAPITALIZATION:
  Capitalize the name of a political party.
    Example: Does she belong to the **Republican Party**?

1. is the democratic party meeting at uncle don's house?

PUNCTUATION:

2. The baby took a bite of food smiled and spit it out

PARTS OF SPEECH: ADVERBS
  Circle the correct word:

3. Don't talk so (loud, loudly).

PARTS OF SPEECH: VERBS
  Some verbs can serve as either a helping verb or a main verb.
  Write <u>HV</u> if the boldfaced verb is a helping verb; write <u>MV</u> if the boldfaced verb is a main verb:

4. A. ____ These nails **are** rusty.   C. ____ I **was** told the truth.
   B. ____ These pots **are** made of clay.   D. ____ I **was** not at home.

SPELLING:
  Write the correct spelling of these words:

5. A. slurp + ing - _____
   B. capture + ed - _____
   C. swim + ing - _____

SENTENCE COMBINING:

6. Most butterflies fly by day.
   Most moths fly by night.

_____

_____

DAY 51

CAPITALIZATION:

1. the butcher's shop is south of pebble shoe company on royal street.

PUNCTUATION:
An appositive is a noun or noun phrase that explains another word beside it. Use a comma before an appositive if it ends a sentence.
Example: Please hand this to my mother, **the woman in the pink suit.**

2. This package is for Tate R Trainer the towns only doctor

PARTS OF SPEECH: ADJECTIVES
Circle any adjective that describes:

3. She pulled a small, woolen hat over her black curly hair.

SUBJECT/VERB:
Underline the subject once and the verb twice:

4. Several people in the park stopped and watched the playful puppies.

SPELLING:
Remember: **A word ending in vowel + consonant + e usually drops the e when adding a suffix beginning with a vowel. A word ending in vowel + consonant + e usually does not drop the e when adding a suffix beginning with a consonant.**
Examples: time + ing = tim**ing**
time + ly = tim**ely**
Write the correct spelling of these words:

5. A.   late + ly - _____
   B.   line + ing - _____
   C.   skim + er - _____

SENTENCE COMBINING:

6. A camel is a ruminant.
   A ruminant chews its cud.

_____

_____

DAY 52

CAPITALIZATION:

1. is rockefeller center near lincoln tunnel in manhattan, new york?

PUNCTUATION:

2. Take me with you   Kendra demanded

PARTS OF SPEECH: ADVERBS
   Circle any adverbs that tell *where, when,* or *how*:

3. Ian said restlessly, "Let's go somewhere later."

PARTS OF SPEECH: VERBS
   Write the contraction:

4. A. he is - _____
    B. we will - _____
    C. were not - _____
    D. you are - _____
    E. they have - _____
    F. I shall - _____

ANALOGIES:
   Circle the correct answer:

5. famed : well-known :: concealed : _____
    (a) sealed   (b) hidden   (c) weapon   (d) open

SENTENCE COMBINING:

6. Jason and Hope ran five miles.
    They were tired.

    _____

    _____

DAY 53

CAPITALIZATION:

1. have you been to bow lake in southeastern new hampshire?

PUNCTUATION:

2. Boat Rules   Do not go beyond chained area
                         Hold on while moving around

PARTS OF SPEECH: PRONOUNS

    If <u>we</u> or <u>us</u> stands beside a noun, cross out the noun and choose the correct pronoun.

       Example: Please stay with (we, us) friends during the football game.

                   Please stay with (we, **us**) ~~friends~~ during the football game.

Circle the correct pronoun:

3. (We, Us) teammates have to decide.

PARTS OF SPEECH: ADJECTIVES/ADVERBS

    Circle the correct word:

4. Janet and Brian draw animals (good, well).

ANALOGIES:

    Circle the correct answer:

5. noisy : quiet :: fragile : _____
    (a) sturdy   (b) delicate   (c) glass   (d) breakable

SENTENCE COMBINING:

6. Christina's sister is a waitress.
    Christina's sister works at a Mexican food restaurant.

_____

_____

DAY 54

CAPITALIZATION:

1. did john adams help to ratify the declaration of independence?

PUNCTUATION:

2. Ill need the following snacks   crackers apples and sunflower seeds

PARTS OF SPEECH: PRONOUNS
   Circle the correct pronoun:

3. Please let (we, us) girls look through your telescope.

PARTS OF SPEECH: ADJECTIVES
   When a linking verb such as *to taste, to smell,* or *to look* is used in a sentence and *was or were* can replace it, use <u>good</u>, not well.

                                    was
   Example: The hot chocolate <u>smelled</u> good.

   Replace the linking verb with *was* or *were*; circle the correct word:

4. That sticky bun looks (good, well).

ANALOGIES:
   Circle the correct answer:

5. ugly : attractive :: trusting : _____
   (a) trust   (b) suspicious   (c) sneaky   (d) deliberate

SENTENCE COMBINING:

6. Lance was happy with his grades.
   Lance threw his report card into the air.

   _____

   _____

DAY 55

CAPITALIZATION:

1. the members of the new haven german club planted trees on labor day.

PUNCTUATION:
   Use underlining or quotation marks:

2. A. Beautiful Brown Eyes (title of a song)   B. Town Tribune (name of a newspaper)

PARTS OF SPEECH: VERBS
   Present tense tells what *is* or what *is happening* now.
      Example: I want a hot dog.
   Past tense tells past time.   Example: Jen blew glass in her studio.
   Future tense tells something that will happen.
      Example: It will snow in the mountains today.

Write PR if the tense is present, write PT if the tense is past, and write FT if the tense is future.

3. A. _____ The book show lasted four hours.
   B. _____ My grandmother will ski with us.
   C. _____ Barry cooks in his spare time.

PARTS OF SPEECH: NOUNS
   Write C if the noun is common; write P if the noun is proper:

4. A. ____ CHRISTMAS   B. ____ CELEBRATION   C. ____ PARADE

ANALOGIES:
   Circle the correct answer:

5. rely : depend :: observe : _____
   (a) find   (b) serve   (c) claim   (d) see

SENTENCE COMBINING:

6. Chandra lifted the garbage lid.
   Chandra saw a snake.
   Chandra screamed.

_____

_____

DAY 56

CAPITALIZATION:
Capitalize the name of a government body.
Example: The **U. S. C**ongress must approve all treaties.

1. the u. s. house of representatives meets today.

PUNCTUATION:

2. Please take this to the teachers workroom said Miss Krupa

PHRASES/CLAUSES:
A phrase is a group of words.
Example: across the bridge
A clause contains a subject and a verb.
Examples: This <u>topping</u> <u>is</u> fat free.
When <u>he</u> <u>was</u> ten years old
Write P if the words form a phrase; write C if the words form a clause:
3. A. _____ Cheering loudly for their team.
   B. _____ Your umbrella is in the closet.

PARTS OF SPEECH: ADJECTIVES
Circle the correct adjective:

4. These enchiladas become (hotter, hottest) when heated a second time.

ANALOGIES:
Circle the correct answer:

5. relay : race :: penny : _____
   (a) nickel   (b) Lincoln   (c) pound   (d) coin

SENTENCE COMBINING:

6. Juan is rather quiet.
   His brother is loud and boisterous.

_____

_____

DAY 57

CAPITALIZATION:

1. take constitution avenue to be near to the lincoln memorial in washington, d. c.

PUNCTUATION:

2. Is the girls club located at 909 W Van Riper Road Montvale NJ   07645

SENTENCE TYPES:
The four sentence types are declarative, interrogative, imperative, and exclamatory.
Write the sentence type:

3. A. _____ Bach was a famous composer.
   B. _____ Have you seen the Tower of London?
   C. _____ Don't tickle me.

PARTS OF SPEECH: NOUNS

Nouns ending in *ff* usually add *s*.   muff - muffs
Nouns ending in *f* may add *s*; however, some change the *f* to *v* and add *es*.   leaf - leaves   **Consult a dictionary if you are uncertain.**
Place a √ if the noun adds s:

4. A. ___ puff   B. ___ loaf   C. ___ whiff   D. ___ chief

SPELLING:
Write the correct spelling of these words:

5. A. amaze + ment - _____
   B. rude + ly - _____
   C. compose + ing - _____

SENTENCE COMBINING:

6. Most volcanoes lie in a zone called "Ring of Fire."
   This is near the edge of the Pacific Ocean.

_____

_____

DAY 58

CAPITALIZATION:

1. in reading class, we discussed "sea fever" by john masefield.

PUNCTUATION:

2. This pantry we believe needs to be stocked with the following soup rice and tuna

CLAUSES:
   All clauses contain a SUBJECT and a VERB.
   An independent clause expresses a complete thought and can stand alone.   Example: <u>We</u> <u>sat</u> on the pier for an hour.
   A dependent clause does not express a complete thought.
         Example: After the basketball <u>team</u> <u>ran</u> onto the court
  Write <u>IC</u> if the clause is independent; write <u>DC</u> if the clause is dependent:
3. A. _____   Where we could see a hole in the fence.
   B. _____   It rains frequently in Princeville in January.

PARTS OF SPEECH: ADVERBS
   Circle the correct adverb:

4. His twin bowls (better, best) than he.

SPELLING:

   Write the correct spelling of these words:

5. A. present + er - _____
   B. meet + ing - _____
   C. debate + or - _____

SENTENCE COMBINING:

6. Erosion can be caused by water.
   Erosion can be caused by wind.
   Erosion can be caused by ice.

DAY 59

CAPITALIZATION:
Capitalize the first two lines of the poem, "Birches":

1. when i see birches bend left to right
   across the line of straighter darker trees

PUNCTUATION:

2. Tonys sister lives at 2 Southwest 5th Street Miami FL   33135

PREFIXES/ROOTS/SUFFIXES:
A root is a base from which words are formed. Some roots can stand alone as a word; some form only a part of a word.
Port is from the Latin word, *portare*, which means to bear or carry.
Using this information, explain the word, *transport*:

3. _____

SUBJECT/VERB:
Underline the subject once and the verb or verb phrase twice:

4. A vegetable tray and a carrot cake have been ordered for the party.

ANALOGIES:
Circle the correct answer:

5. newspaper : classifieds :: wheel : _____
   (a) round   (b) spoke   (c) convertible   (d) jeep

SENTENCE COMBINING:

6. Mother is trying to light the grill.
   The charcoal won't ignite.

_____

_____

DAY 60

CAPITALIZATION:

1. "is gypsum cave near nelles air force base?" asked kyla.

PUNCTUATION:

2. Mrs Orwigs name was listed on the commencement list as Orwig Lali

FRIENDLY LETTER ENVELOPES:

3. _____

    Tami Begay
    10 Modesto Way
    Shippensburg, PA   17257

                       Julian Vargas
                       920 Deer Crossing Drive
                       Flagstaff, AZ   86101

   A. What is the zip code of the person sending this letter? _____
   B. What is the last name of the person receiving this letter? _____

PARTS OF SPEECH:

   Circle the correct word:

4. He (don't, doesn't) like to go to the zoo.

ANALOGIES:

   Circle the correct answer:

5. pen : writing :: hammer : _____
   (a) claw   (b) tool   (c) pounding   (d) carpenter

SENTENCE COMBINING:

6. Linda wants to go to Alaska.
   She wants to go with her friends.
   She wants to go this summer.

_____

_____

DAY 61

CAPITALIZATION:

1. did grandpa go aboard the u. s. s. constitution docked in boston?

PUNCTUATION:

2.   12235 Pleasant Street
                                 Salem MA 01970
                                 January 27 20--
   Dear Cal
       Our new rug has an unusual design and is woven
                                 Your uncle
                                 Rafe

FRIENDLY LETTERS:
Use the letter in #2 to answer these questions:

3. A. What part of a friendly letter is *Dear Cal*? _____
    B. What part of a friendly letter is *Your uncle*? _____

DICTIONARY SKILLS: ALPHATBETIZING
Write these words in alphabetical order:

4. jade   bath   jar   forest   jail   bass   earn

SIMPLE/COMPOUND/COMPLEX SENTENCES:
A simple sentence has a subject and a verb.
        Example: <u>He</u> <u>peeled</u> potatoes for dinner.
A simple sentence may have a compound subject or a compound verb.
        Example: <u>He</u> and his <u>grandfather</u> <u>peeled</u> potatoes for dinner.
Write a simple sentence:

5. _____

SENTENCE COMBINING:

6. Joy went to the pharmacy.
   Her prescription was not ready.

_____

_____

DAY 62

CAPITALIZATION:

1. salton sea is near california's chocolate mountains.

PUNCTUATION:

2. Mario asked Wheres Parkers picture

PARTS OF SPEECH: ADJECTIVES/ADVERBS
Real is usually an adjective meaning true, sincere, or genuine.
Really is an adverb that tells *to what extent*.

Circle the correct word:
3. A. Poppa gave us a (real, really) gold coin.
   B. I am (real, really) tired.

PARTS OF SPEECH: VERBS
Circle the correct verb:
4. A. She must have (given, gave) us the wrong address.
   B. A jar of salsa had (fell, fallen) from the pantry shelf.

SPELLING:
A word ending in consonant + y usually changes the y to i before adding a suffix beginning with a vowel. However, many words do not drop the y when adding ing.
   Examples: try + ed = tried   try + ing = trying

Write the correct spelling of these words:
5. A. study + ed - _____
   B. study + ing - _____
   C. study + s - _____

SENTENCE COMBINING:

6. Eyeballs are protected by bony structures.
   These bony structures are called orbits.

   _____

   _____

DAY 63

CAPITALIZATION:
Capitalize this outline:
1.   i. mineral resources
   - a. oil
   - b. coal

   ii. other resources

PUNCTUATION:

2. Jana asked Arent your parents from Finland Kami

PARTS OF SPEECH: VERBS
Write a √ if the verb is regular:

3. A. ____ to stop   B. ____ to pour   C. ____ to bring   D. ____ to try

PARTS OF SPEECH: PRONOUNS
A pronoun takes the place of a noun.
Me him, her, us, them, you, whom, and *it* can serve as an object.

Write an appropriate pronoun:

4. Do you want to go with _____?

SPELLING:
Write the correct spelling of these words:

5. A. rely + ed - _____

   B. rely + ing - _____

   C. fry + ing - _____

SENTENCE COMBINING:

6. The toddler is screaming.
   The child does not want to take a nap.
   His mother is ignoring him.

_____

_____

DAY 64

CAPITALIZATION:
  Capitalize this heading and greeting of a friendly letter:

1.
                                        12 north perry drive
                                        fort worth, tx   76133
                                        november 3, 20--

    dear anne,

PUNCTUATION:

2. Yes my mother or my aunt will present a slide show on Tuesday Feb 12

PARTS OF SPEECH: NOUNS
  Write C if the noun is concrete; write A if the noun is abstract:

3. A. _____ staple   B. _____ kindness   C. _____ respect

SENTENCES/FRAGMENTS/RUN-ONS:
  Write S if the words form a sentence; write F for fragment if the words do not form a sentence:

4. A. _____ The creek spilled over its banks.
    B. _____ The fuse box in the garage.

ANALOGIES:
  Circle the correct answer:

5. forget : remember :: strict : _____
    (a) forceful   (b) apparent   (c) lenient   (d) disciplined

SENTENCE COMBINING:

6. Mark wore a tie.
    It was a pink tie.
    It was a silk tie.
    He wore it with a black suit.
    He was attending his cousin's wedding.

_____

_____

DAY 65

CAPITALIZATION:
Capitalize these titles:
1. A. the fence post
   B. colorado history for kids
   C. "she walks in beauty"

PUNCTUATION:
Punctuate this outline:
2. I Snakes
      A Rattlesnakes
      B Cobras
   II Lizards

PARTS OF SPEECH: ADVERBS
Some adverbs tell *to what extent*. Seven adverbs often tell *to what extent: not, so, very, too, quite, rather, and somewhat.* There are others such as *extremely* and *really*.

Write an adverb that tells *to what extent*:

3. The wind blew _____ briskly through the canyon.

PARTS OF SPEECH: NOUNS
Write the possessive:
4. a pet belonging to that family: _____

ANALOGIES:
Circle the correct answer:
5. trimester : three :: quadruplet : _____
   (a) two   (b) ten   (c) four   (d) six

SENTENCE COMBINING:
6. This stuffed giraffe is musical.
   This giraffe is yellow.
   This giraffe belongs to a baby.

   _____

   _____

DAY 66

CAPITALIZATION:

1. "the african people love their land," said professor shand.

PUNCTUATION:

2. Yes Allen were leaving for Hyattsville at two oclock this afternoon

PARTS OF SPEECH: NOUNS
   Plural means more than one.
   Place a √ if the noun adds es to form the plural:

3. A. ___ birch   D. ___ shell   G. ___ fizz
   B. ___ splash   E. ___ loss   H. ___ charm
   C. ___ fix   F. ___ mess   I. ___ Christmas

SUBJECT/VERB:
   Underline the subject; circle the verb that agrees with the subject:

4. Our team (is, are) in the finals.

ANALOGIES:
   Circle the correct answer:

5. response : answer :: banner : _____
   (a) computer   (b) advertising   (c) pennant   (d) teasing

SENTENCE COMBINING:

6. Lightning struck the tree.
   The tree split at its base.

   _____

   _____

DAY 67

CAPITALIZATION:

1. did king henry VIII of england have a warship named the <u>mary rose</u>?

PUNCTUATION:

2. Jordans family rode on an outrigger a type of canoe used on the ocean

PREFIXES/ROOTS/SUFFIXES:

Prefixes help to understand word meaning:

sub - under (**sub**zero) **pro - forward** (**pro**cession)
re - again (**re**model); **back**wards (**re**treat) **hyper - overly** (**hyper**active)

Write an appropriate prefix:

3. A. Our bean sprout is _____merged in water.

   B. She put the car in _____verse.

   C. My skin is _____sensitive.

   D. You may _____ceed.

PARTS OF SPEECH: NOUNS

Circle any nouns:

4. The floats in the parade were displayed in a park near a large statue.

ANALOGIES:

Circle the correct answer:

5. costly : inexpensive :: fake : _____
   (a) rare   (b) false   (c) authentic   (d) fur

SENTENCE COMBINING:

6. Maria's mother likes opera.
   Maria's father does not like opera.

DAY 68

CAPITALIZATION:

Capitalize these lines of poetry by Robert Frost:

1. the rain to the wind said,
   "you push and i'll pelt."

PUNCTUATION:

2. Yes Id love a strawberry filled ice cream cone   declared Mona

PARTS OF SPEECH: VERBS

Circle the correct verb:

3. A. The newspaper is (lying, laying) in the driveway.
   B. Ellen has (boughten, bought) a motorcycle.
   C. Michael had (shook, shaken) his head in protest.

WORDS:

Circle the correct word:

4. A. (May, Can) you drive a car with standard transmission?
   B. I know that (they're, there, their) not hungry yet.
   C. The (to, two, too) year old wants a snack, (to, two, too).

ANALOGIES:

Circle the correct answer:

5. tourist : traveler :: wanderer : _____
   (a) hunter   (b) nomad   (c) gatherer   (d) immigrant

SENTENCE COMBINING:

6. The girl was surprised.
   She placed her hand over her mouth.
   She also giggled.

_____

_____

DAY 69

CAPITALIZATION:

1. we went to galveston, texas, on the gulf of mexico.

PUNCTUATION:
   Place a comma after <u>two</u> prepositional phrases that begin a sentence.
   Example: *With the help of two friends,* we were able to load our van.
   Place a comma after one <u>long</u> prepositional phrase that begins a sentence. Example: *After the very disturbing news,* everyone grew quiet.

2. After the babys christening the family gathered at the sister in laws home for lunch

PARTS OF SPEECH: CONJUNCTIONS
   Write a sentence containing a coordinating conjunction:

3. _____

PARTS OF SPEECH: ADVERBS
   Circle any adverbs that tell *how*:

4. Dakota worked quickly but carefully.

SIMPLE/COMPOUND/COMPLEX SENTENCES:
   A complex sentence may have one complete thought (independent clause) and one or more incomplete thoughts (dependent clauses).
   Example: Before <u>we went</u> to the lake, <u>we packed</u> a lunch.
                 dependent clause   independent clause
   Finish each complex sentence.

5. A. When I was five years old, _____

   B. After we watched a movie, _____

SENTENCE COMBINING:

6. Venus is the second planet from the sun.
   Venus is a rocky planet.

   _____

   _____

DAY 70

CAPITALIZATION:

Capitalize this outline:

1. i. types of apartments
    a. furnished
    b. unfurnished
   ii. types of houses

PUNCTUATION:

Write the abbreviation:

2. A. United States - _____   B. meter - _____   C. quart - _____

PARTS OF SPEECH: PRONOUNS
Circle the correct pronoun:

3. The small child planned to startle Toby and (she, her) by jumping out at them.

PHRASES/CLAUSES:
   A phrase is a group of words.   Example: under the pillow
   A clause contains a subject and a verb.
      Example: If Mr. Haines leaves early
   Write P if the words form a phrase; write C if the words form a clause:

4. A. _____ After you finish your homework
   B. _____ After the second quarter

ANALOGIES:

Circle the correct answer:

5. flock : sheep :: pack : _____
   (a) travel   (b) luggage   (c) wolf   (d) ram

SENTENCE COMBINING:

6. A small blue jay hopped around the patio.
   The blue jay had a twig in its beak.

   _____

   _____

DAY 71

CAPITALIZATION:

1. let's go to woodbury mall near chippenham parkway in richmond.

PUNCTUATION:

2. The winner by the way hasnt been decided Noah

CLAUSES:
   All clauses contain a SUBJECT and a VERB.
   An independent clause expresses a complete thought and can stand alone.   Example: My <u>foot</u> <u>was caught</u> between the sofa and a chair.
   A dependent clause does not express a complete thought.
       Example: Before <u>I begin</u> my homework
   Write IC if the clause is independent; write DC if the clause is dependent:

3. A. _____ Moses created a ceramic dish.
    B. _____ If you enter by the back door.

PARTS OF SPEECH: VERBS
   Circle the correct verb:

4. One of the boys (speak, speaks) French.

ANALOGIES:
   Circle the correct answer:

5. Salt Lake City : Utah :: Santa Fe : _____
    (a) Phoenix   (b) Mexico   (c) Southwest   (d) New Mexico

SENTENCE COMBINING:

6. Jina's head hurts.
    She bumped her head on the car door.

    _____

    _____

DAY 72

CAPITALIZATION:

1. is jones bay near croatan national forest in north carolina?

PUNCTUATION:

2. Their grandparents anniversary I assume is next Wednesday July 7

PARTS OF SPEECH: ADVERBS
Unscramble these adverbs that tell *to what extent:*

3. A. nto - _____   E. ahrter - _____
   B. os - _____   F. wsoaemht - _____
   C. oot - _____   G. iuteq - _____
   D. yevr - _____

SUBJECTS/VERBS:
In an imperative sentence, the subject is often not stated. It is understood to be *you*.
   Example: Sit here.   (You) Sit here.
Underline the subject once and the verb twice:

4. Wait for me.

ANALOGIES:
The first two words of an analogy may express a male - female (or female - male) relationship. The third word and the answer must show the same relationship.   Example: Hen : rooster :: doe : _____
                    (a) fawn   **(b) buck**   (c) habitat   (d) Bambi

   Circle the correct answer:

5. mare : stallion :: ewe : _____
   (a) sheep   (b) lamb   (c) wool   (d) ram

SENTENCE COMBINING:

6. They drove on Interstate 70 for ten miles.
   Then, they took a county road to a cabin.

   _____

   _____

DAY 73

CAPITALIZATION:

1. yesterday, beth's friend, who lives in the southwest, broke out with german measles.

PUNCTUATION:
   Place a dash (the width of M) or parentheses ( ) to provide additional information.
   Example: Mora scrubbed walls -- very dirty ones.
              Mora scrubbed walls (very dirty ones).

2. He did it purposely   to prove a point

DICTIONARY SKILLS: GUIDE WORDS
   Two guide words appear in boldfaced type at the top of each dictionary page. The first word listed is the first entry on that page. The second word is the last entry on that page.
   Place a √ if the word will appear on a page with the guide words:

   tourist - turn:

3. A. ___ towel   B. ___ train   C. ___ tune   D. ___ tool

PARTS OF SPEECH: VERBS
   Underline the subject once and the verb or verb phrase twice:

4. During the ice storm, the police and road crews helped stranded motorists.

ANALOGIES:
   Circle the correct answer:

5. poet : poetess :: actor : _____
   (a) drama   (b) actress   (c) television   (d) cinema

SENTENCE COMBINING:

6. American football is played with eleven players.
   Canadian football is played with twelve players.

DAY 74

CAPITALIZATION:

1. governor brinwood, a republican, spoke at a gooseberry inn luncheon.

PUNCTUATION:

2. Their new son I think is being dedicated on Sunday April 30

SUBJECT/VERB:
   Underline the subject once and the verb twice:

3. The child took his mother's hand and crossed the lane.

PARTS OF SPEECH: ADJECTIVES/ADVERBS
   Circle the correct word:

4. Hot cinnamon rolls taste (good, well) early in the morning.

SPELLING:
   A word ending in consonant + y usually changes y to i when adding a suffix beginning with a consonant.   Example: happy + ness = happiness
   Write the correct spelling of these words:

5. A. lazy + ness - _____
   B. merry + ment - _____
   C. icy + ly - _____

SENTENCE COMBINING:

6. Treasure maps were handed out.
   The children began to search.
   They were looking for a metal box.

   _____

   _____

DAY 75

CAPITALIZATION:

1. a polynesian lady served us hawaiian chicken at luau restaurant.

PUNCTUATION:

2. Angelo exclaimed Wow What a view

PARTS OF SPEECH: VERBS
   Write the contraction:

3. A. does not - _____   D. will not - _____
   B. there is - _____   E. I have - _____
   C. they are - _____   F. should not - _____

PARTS OF SPEECH: ADJECTIVES/ADVERBS
   Circle the correct word:

4. This tape doesn't stick (good, well).

SPELLING:
   Remember: A word ending in consonant + y usually changes y to i when adding a suffix except when adding the suffix ing.
   Examples: fry + ed = fried   fry + ing = frying
   Write the correct spelling of these words:

5. A. comply + ance - _____
   B. steady + ly - _____
   C. cry + ing - _____

SENTENCE COMBINING:

6. Jim used his new metal detector.
   He found a soda can.
   He found several coins.
   He found a child's shovel.

_____

_____

DAY 76

CAPITALIZATION:

1. during the space age, neil armstrong walked on the moon.

PUNCTUATION:
Place a comma before a title if it ends a sentence.
   Example: Their professor is Kammie Rivera, Ph.D.

2. Both of his sisters employer is Noah B Troon D D S

PARTS OF SPEECH: ADJECTIVES
Circle any descriptive adjectives:

3. Plush, musical bears were displayed on their soft, leather sofa.

SYNONYMS/ANTONYMS/HOMONYMS:
**Homonyms are words that sound alike but are spelled differently.
Synonyms are words that have similar meanings.
Antonyms are words with opposite meanings.**

Write H if the words are homonyms, S if the words are synonyms, and A if the words are antonyms:

4. A. ___ pare - trim   B. ___ pare - pair   C. ___ pare - increase

ANALOGIES:
Circle the correct answer:

5. infinite : endless :: dissimilar : _____
   (a) similar   (b) unlike   (c) difficult   (d) finite

SENTENCE COMBINING:

6. His skin is very fair.
   He burns easily.

_____

_____

DAY 77

CAPITALIZATION:

1. the town of wales, alaska, is on the bering strait.

PUNCTUATION:
Use underlining or quotation marks:

2. A. Boating (title of a magazine)
   B. Healthy Eating Habits (title of a magazine article)
   C. Other Skies (name of a book)

PARTS OF SPEECH: VERBS

Place a √ if the sentence contains a verb phrase (helping verb):

Hint: You may want to delete any prepositional phrases, underline the subject once and the verb or verb phrase twice.

3. A. ___ They are going to Alaska.
   B. ___ These moccasins are unusual.

PREFIXES/ROOTS/SUFFIXES:
Tion is a suffix that means action or process.
Using this information, explain the word, *completion:*

4. _____

SPELLING:
Words that end in vowel + y usually do not change when adding a suffix.   Examples: pray + ed = prayed   key + ed = keyed
Write the correct spelling of these words:

5. A. destroy + ing - _____
   B. pay + ment - _____
   C. replay + ed - _____

SENTENCE COMBINING:

6. The grandmother bathed the baby.
   The grandmother laughed at the baby's silly faces.

_____

_____

DAY 78

CAPITALIZATION:

1. did michelangelo, an artist, do a marble sculpture called <u>the rebel slave</u>?

PUNCTUATION:
   Place a comma after <u>two</u> prepositional phrases that begin a sentence.
   Example: *Before the beginning of the game,* the team warmed up.
   Place a comma after one <u>long</u> prepositional phrase that begins a sentence. Example: *From that highest mountain,* we can see the ocean.

2. At the end of the month Julies mom always balances her checkbook

PARTS OF SPEECH: VERBS
   Write <u>PR</u> if the tense is *present*, write <u>PT</u> if the tense is *past*, and write <u>FT</u> if the tense is *future*.

3. A. _____ The tram will arrive in ten minutes.
    B. _____ They send humorous cards to their parents.
    C. _____ The phone rang for five minutes.

PARTS OF SPEECH: ADJECTIVES
   Circle the correct adjective:

4. Of the various antique dishes, this cake plate, I think, is (older, oldest).

SPELLING:
   Write the correct spelling of these words:

5. A. obey + ed - _____
    B. silly + ness - _____
    C. boy + ish - _____

SENTENCE COMBINING:

6. Patty's eyes are large.
    Patty's eyes are blue.
    Patty's eyes are very expressive.

    _____

    _____

DAY 79

CAPITALIZATION:
Capitalize this friendly letter:

1.
                        921 banyan trail
                        boca raton, fl 33431   **(A)**
                        october 12, 20--

    dear aunt sharon,   **(B)**

        have you researched the old coin that we found?   **(C)**

                           your nephew,   **(D)**
                           mike   **(E)**

PUNCTUATION:

2. David cant go with us because his brother in law is visiting from Dayton Ohio

FRIENDLY LETTER:
Label the parts of the above friendly letter:

3. A. _____   D. _____
    B. _____   E. _____
    C. _____

PARTS OF SPEECH: PREPOSITIONS
Cross out any prepositional phrases; underline the subject once and the verb or verb phrase twice:

4. On a very clear night, we looked at the moon through our telescope.

SPELLING:
Write the correct spelling of these words:

5. A. response + ive - _____

    B. lace + y - _____

    C. pretty + ly - _____

SENTENCE COMBINING:

6. Tara volunteers several hours a week.
   Tara is a candy striper at a local hospital.

_____

_____

DAY 80

CAPITALIZATION:

1. is the islamic religion also referred to as moslem?

PUNCTUATION:

2. Dear Jemima
    You asked about Nick and Annes wedding They were married on Sunday December 24 2000
    Trena

PARTS OF SPEECH: NOUNS

Write <u>C</u> if the noun is common; write <u>P</u> if the noun is proper:

3. A. ____ GAME   B. ____ CHESS   C. ____ OLYMPICS

PARTS OF SPEECH: PREPOSITIONS

Circle any prepositional phrases; box any object of the preposition:

4. His glasses are on the table by the front door.

ANALOGIES:

The first two words may express cause and effect. The first word states the cause; the second states the result or effect. Therefore, the third word must express a cause; the answer must reflect the result or effect of that.

Example: Decay : cavity :: rain : _____.
(a) water   (b) chilliness   (c) drizzle   **(d) dampness**

Decay causes a *cavity* in teeth; *rain* causes *dampness*.

Circle the correct answer:

5. laceration : pain :: fire : _____
    (a) heat   (b) fuel   (c) ignite   (d) camping

SENTENCE COMBINING:

6. The trireme was a type of ship used in 400 A. D.
    It was powered by 170 oarsmen.

_____

_____

DAY 81

CAPITALIZATION:

1. the explorer, magellan, rounded cape horn at the tip of south america.

PUNCTUATION:
If part of a sentence occurs after a city and state, place a comma also after the state.
  Example: Did you ever go to Shreveport, Louisiana, with your parents?

2. Ive always wanted to go to Kansas City Missouri to see my cousins

PARTS OF SPEECH: ADVERBS
Circle any adverbs that tell *to what extent:*

3. Although the child seems rather ill, her fever is not very high.

PARTS OF SPEECH: VERBS
Write the contraction:

4. A. you will - _____
   B. I would - _____
   C. were not - _____
   D. what is - _____
   E. I am - _____
   F. you are - _____

ANALOGIES:
Circle the correct answer:

5. game : enjoyment :: tornado : _____
   (a) pressure   (b) cyclone   (c) destruction   (d) hurricane

SENTENCE COMBINING:

6. The wind blew strongly.
   Waves smashed against the rocks.

_____

_____

DAY 82

CAPITALIZATION:

Capitalize these titles:

1. A. ultimate visual dictionary
   B. "in the early morning"
   C. "autos and their owners"

PUNCTUATION:

2. Prepared for the worst Mona marched into her supervisors office

PARTS OF SPEECH: PRONOUNS

Possessive pronouns show ownership.
Possessive pronouns are: my, mine   our, ours   it, its
                          his   their, theirs
                          her, hers   your, yours

Write an appropriate possessive pronoun:

3. Jana went hiking with _____ dog.

SENTENCE TYPES:

Write the sentence type:

4. A. _____ This is hot!
   B. _____ Hand me the mop.
   C. _____ Will you hand me the mop?

ANALOGIES:

Circle the correct answer:

5. disease : nausea :: earthquake : _____
   (a) time   (b) stabilizing   (c) movement   (d) California

SENTENCE COMBINING:

6. The moon is the only natural satellite of the Earth.
   The moon takes 27.3 days to rotate around the Earth.

_____

_____

DAY 83

CAPITALIZATION:

1. were german submarines used during world war I?

PUNCTUATION:

2.
                              Post Office Box 25022
                              Madison WI   53701
                              March 4 20--
  Dear Joy
       Matt Chrissy and I bought a new horse last night
                              Your niece
                              Lucy

PARTS OF SPEECH: PRONOUNS
Circle the correct pronoun:

3. During the debate, (we, us) students had to pay close attention to each speaker.

SENTENCE TYPES:
Change this interrogative sentence to an exclamatory one:

   Will you stop that?

4. _____

SPELLING:
Remember: Words ending in vowel + vowel + consonant (VVC) do not usually change when adding a suffix.   Example: greet + er = greeter
        Words ending in consonant + consonant + <u>e</u> (CCe) usually drop the <u>e</u> when adding a suffix beginning with a vowel.
               Example: huddle + ing = huddling

Write the correct spelling of these words:

5. A.   demand + ing - _____
   B.   coil + ing - _____
   C.   rust + ic - _____

SENTENCE COMBINING:

6. The model has shiny white teeth.
   The model's smile dazzles everyone.

_____

DAY 84

CAPITALIZATION:

1. the british architect, sir joseph paxton, built london's famous crystal palace.

PUNCTUATION:

2. Can koi a type of tropical fish live to be over two hundred years old

PARTS OF SPEECH: VERBS
   Circle the correct verb:

3. A. Mr. Brody has not (brung, brought) his camera.

   B. Someone may have (written, wrote) the secret code.

   C. That diver has (swum, swam) since she was three years old.

CLAUSES:
   A clause contains a subject and a verb.
   An independent clause expresses a complete thought.
      Example: He always gargles for thirty seconds.
   A dependent clause does not express a complete thought.
      Example: Before the new hotel was built
   Write IC if the clause is independent; write DC if the clause is dependent:

4. A. _____ When the sun slid behind a cloud in the middle of the afternoon.

   B. _____ Their hands were chapped from the cold and wind.

SPELLING:
   Write the correct spelling of these words:

5. A. flash + ing - _____

   B. paddle + ed - _____

   C. bubble + ing - _____

SENTENCE COMBINING:

6. Alana is a photographer.
   She specializes in children's portraits.

   _____

   _____

DAY 85

CAPITALIZATION:

1. during the revolutionary war, samuel adams led the boston tea party.

PUNCTUATION:

2. Havent you ever met these triplets Nick Nicole and Nina

PARTS OF SPEECH: NOUNS
Write the possessive:

3. a quilt belonging to Grandmother: _____

PREFIXES/ROOTS/SUFFIXES:
A root is a base from which words are formed. Some roots can stand alone as a word; some form only a part of a word.
Equine is from the Latin word *equus* meaning horse.

4. If someone mentions that he will be spending the day with his equine friend, he would probably be spending it _____.

SPELLING:
Write the correct spelling of these words:

5. A. baby + ed - _____
   B. baby + ing - _____
   C. strap + ing - _____

SENTENCE COMBINING:

6. The rain ceased in the early morning.
   The sun shone for the rest of the day.

_____

_____

DAY 86

CAPITALIZATION:

1. the poet, henry wadsworth longfellow, was a professor at bowdoin college in maine.

PUNCTUATION:

2. Well these rocks of course arent valuable   said Cam mildly

DICTIONARY SKILLS: ALPHATBETIZING
   Write these words in alphabetical order:

3. story   paste   stare   track   pasta   range

PARTS OF SPEECH: NOUNS
   An indirect object is the receiver of *some* direct objects. You can insert <u>to</u> or <u>for</u> mentally before an indirect object.

                                       to   I.O.   D.O.
   Example: Mario handed / the customer a sundae.

   Underline the subject once and the verb or verb phrase twice. Label the direct object - <u>D.O.</u> and the indirect object - <u>I.O.</u>:

4. The postal worker sold me a special stamp.

ANALOGIES:
   Circle the correct answer:

5. bride : wife :: groom : _____
   (a) horse   (b) father   (c) usher   (d) husband

SENTENCE COMBINING:

6. Ellis Island is in the harbor of New York.
   It once was an examination center for immigrants to America.

   _____

   _____

DAY 87

CAPITALIZATION:

1. having developed pneumonia, she entered nordic medical center last february.

PUNCTUATION:

2. Ive mentioned that youre not pleased with their decision   said Mrs Korte

PARTS OF SPEECH: CONJUNCTIONS/INTERJECTIONS
   Box any interjections; circle any coordinating conjunctions:

3. Whew! That car slid on ice but it didn't hit the chunky post or the tree!

SENTENCES/FRAGMENTS/RUN-ONS:

   Write S if the words form a sentence; write F for fragment if the words do not form a sentence:

4. A. _____ Chessa and I rarely that.
   B. _____ Please don't mumble.

ANALOGIES:

   Circle the correct answer:

5. flashlight : illuminate :: disinfectant : _____
   (a) purify   (b) infect   (c) fester   (d) disperse

SENTENCE COMBINING:

6. Angling means fishing with a rod.
   Angling also means fishing with a reel.
   It also means fishing with a line.
   It also means fishing with a lure.

   _____

   _____

DAY 88

CAPITALIZATION:

1. on valentine's day, mom and aunt beth gave us misty* marshmallows.

*brand name

PUNCTUATION:

2. No I shouldnt be surprised that her name in the telephone book is listed as Po T K

PARTS OF SPEECH: ADVERBS
   Circle the correct adverb:
3. Lynn spoke (more clearly, most clearly) during her second speech.

PREFIXES/ROOTS/SUFFIXES:
   Prefixes help to understand word meanings:
      pseudo - false (pseudopod)   super - above, highest (superman)
      anti - against (antifreeze)   multi, poly - many (multiply); (polygraph)

   Write an appropriate prefix:

4. A. Their apartment _____intendent had their plumbing fixed.
    B. Another word for a fake name is _____nym.
    C. We like _____grain cereal.
    D. In geometry, the class studies many sided figures or _____gons.

ANALOGIES:
   Circle the correct answer:

5. wrongly : incorrectly :: impulsively : _____
   (a) understanding   (b) forcefully   (c) reluctantly   (d) hastily

SENTENCE COMBINING:

6. A basket of dried flowers fell to the floor.
   The dried flowers crumbled.

_____

_____

DAY 89

CAPITALIZATION:

1. his dad cooked belgian waffles at a lion's club breakfast.

PUNCTUATION:

2. By the way the following streets are closed Ash Place Lazy Lane and Ruby Drive

PARTS OF SPEECH: ADVERBS

Circle any adverbs that tell *how* or *when*:

3. Ty and Chessa played soccer well today.

PARTS OF SPEECH: NOUNS

Nouns ending in *ay, uy, ey,* and *oy* usually add <u>s</u> to form the plural. Nouns ending in consonant + y, usually change the *y* to *i* and add <u>es</u> to form the plural.

Write the plural of each noun:

4. A. jay - _____   D. alloy - _____
   B. donkey - _____   E. guppy - _____
   C. history - _____   F. lullaby - _____

ANALOGIES:

Circle the correct answer:

5. shivering : shaking :: leaning : _____
   (a) skiing   (b) upright   (c) capsizing   (d) sailing

SENTENCE COMBINING:

6. Cuckoos are grayish-brown birds.
   They lay eggs in the nests of other birds.

   _____

   _____

DAY 90

CAPITALIZATION:

1. we drove on natchez trace parkway which originally was a native american trail.

PUNCTUATION:

2. If you agree   said Mrs Leon   please raise your hand

SUBJECT/VERB:

Underline the subject; circle the verb that agrees with the subject:

3. The handles of the chest (needs, need) to be replaced.

PREFIXES/ROOTS/SUFFIXES:

A root is a base from which words are formed. Some roots can stand alone as a word; some form only a part of a word.

Vigor is a Latin root that means make strong.

Write a sentence using the word, *vigorous:*

4. _____

ANALOGIES:

Circle the correct answer:

5. cut : scissors :: paint : _____
   (a) brush   (b) thinner   (c) picture   (d) wall

SENTENCE COMBINING:

6. We can go to the park.
   We must wait until our parents get home.

   _____

   _____

DAY 91

CAPITALIZATION:

1. i. vacation tours
      a. land
         1. bus
         2. train
      b. cruises

PUNCTUATION:

2. Toward the end of winter they visited their aunt in Washington D C

PARTS OF SPEECH: ADJECTIVES/ADVERBS

Real is usually an adjective meaning true, sincere, or genuine.
Really is an adverb that tells *to what extent*.

Circle the correct word:

3. A. They are (real, really) excited about the game?
   B. Is this frame made of (real, really) teakwood?

FRIENDLY LETTERS/ENVELOPES:
Write your return address on this envelope:

4. _____
   _____
   _____
   _____

   _____

ANALOGIES:
Circle the correct answer:

5. jump : pounce :: cry : _____
   (a) sob   (b) tears   (c) laugh   (d) meow

SENTENCE COMBINING:

6. Monkey bread is the fruit of the African baobao tree.
   Monkey bread is eaten by monkeys.

   _____

DAY 92

CAPITALIZATION:
Capitalize these lines of poetry by C. Sandburg:

1. maybe he believes me, maybe not,
   maybe i can marry him, maybe not.

PUNCTUATION:

2. Miss R Poshski
   2396 S Chrysler Dr
   Auburn Hills   MI   48326

PARTS OF SPEECH: NOUNS
Write C if the noun is concrete; write A if the noun is abstract:

3. A. _____ battery   B. _____ bravery   C. _____ sink

PARTS OF SPEECH: ADVERBS
Circle the correct word:

4. I like this pancake syrup, but Yancy never seems to want (none, any).

ANALOGIES:
Circle the correct answer:

5. plunge : dive :: push : _____
   (a) pose   (b) pull   (c) nudge   (d) protest

SENTENCE COMBINING:

6. A waitress served muffins.
   The waitress was from England.
   The waitress spoke with a British accent.

   _____

   _____

DAY 93

CAPITALIZATION:
Capitalize these titles:

1. A. "brilliant britain"
   B. "suburb on the green"
   C. teachers are special

PUNCTUATION:

2. By the end of the third quarter both teams coaches were shouting excitedly

DIRECT OBJECTS:
Underline the subject once and the verb or verb phrase twice. Circle the direct object:
Remember: Deleting prepositional phrases will simplify the sentence.

3. I must have left my package in the car.

PARTS OF SPEECH: VERBS
Place a √ if the verb is regular:

4. A. ____ to find   C. ____ to buy   E. ____ to hide
   B. ____ to fine   D. ____ to cry   F. ____ to ride

ANALOGIES:
Circle the correct answer:

5. cute : gorgeous :: scary : _____
   (a) fearful   (b) afraid   (c) story   (d) terrifying

SENTENCE COMBINING:

6. The child drew a picture.
   He drew a picture of a house.
   The house has two doors and no windows.

_____

_____

DAY 94

CAPITALIZATION:

1. "we played jump rope at penn's park," said molly.

PUNCTUATION:

2. Alli Id like to borrow your long silk scarf for a play

DICTIONARY SKILLS: GUIDE WORDS

Two guide words appear in boldfaced type at the top of each dictionary page. The first word listed is the first entry on that page. The second word is the last entry on that page.

Place a √ if the word will appear on a page with the guide words:
ace - artistic:

3. A. ___ acid   B. ___ artist   C. ___ academy   D. ___ arsenic

CLAUSES:

Write IC if the clause is independent; write DC if the clause is dependent:

4. A. _____ Whenever Briana recites a poem in front of her classmates.
   B. _____ Her cotton gloves were too thin to keep her hands very warm.

ANALOGIES:

Circle the correct answer:

5. mane : horse :: udder : _____
   (a) gland   (b) milk   (c) teat   (d) cow

SENTENCE COMBINING:

6. An ostrich is a swift-running bird.
   An ostrich is the largest bird.
   It is the most powerful bird.

_____

_____

DAY 95

CAPITALIZATION:

1. yesterday, his mother helped to plant dutch tulips in hyde square near hume lane.

PUNCTUATION:

2. The baker answered   No this isnt a three layer cake

PARTS OF SPEECH: **NOUNS**
   Circle any nouns:

3. On Monday, Kam hooked up his printer to his new computer.

PHRASES/CLAUSES:
   A phrase is a group of words.   Example: since Friday
   A clause contains a subject and a verb.
      Examples: Is this pearl real?
                  Alita loves to surf.
   Write P if the words form a phrase; write C if the words form a clause:

4. A. _____ From the very beginning
   B. _____ When Igor began to walk

ANALOGIES:
   Circle the correct answer:

5. crop : wheat :: aircraft : _____
   (a) helicopter   (b) flying   (c) landing   (d) space

SENTENCE COMBINING:

6. The patient waited in the doctor's office for an hour.
   The patient moaned softly.
   The patient was displeased.

   _____

   _____

DAY 96

CAPITALIZATION:

1. during the french and indian war, the iroquois indians helped the british troops.

PUNCTUATION:

2. Deans mother asked   Isnt your brother twenty nine

PARTS OF SPEECH: VERBS
  Circle the correct verb:

3. A. The sun has (risen, rose).
   B. Gusts of wind had (blew, blown) down the chimney.
   C. Have you ever (wore, worn) snowshoes?
   D. Those tomatoes were (grown, grew) in a greenhouse.
   E. Her spirits had (sank, sunk) when she heard the news.

PARTS OF SPEECH: PRONOUNS
  Reflexive pronouns are *myself, himself, herself, yourself, ourselves, themselves,* and *itself*.
  <u>Theirselves</u> and <u>hisself</u> are always incorrect.
  Write an appropriate pronoun:

4. She changed the tire _____.

ANALOGIES:
  Circle the correct answer:

5. heir : heiress :: hero : _____
   (a) knight   (b) heroess   (c) heroine   (d) lady

SENTENCE COMBINING:

6. Diana's doll has a porcelain head.
   Diana's doll is an antique.
   The porcelain head is cracked.

   _____

   _____

DAY 97

CAPITALIZATION:

1. is the english language spoken in the union of south africa?

PUNCTUATION:

2. Brandy youre first on my list   said Tate

PREFIXES/ROOTS/SUFFIXES:
    A suffix is an ending; it is added to a root.
        Ness is a suffix that means *state of or condition of.*
    Using this information, explain the word, *happiness:*

3. _____

PARTS OF SPEECH: ADJECTIVES/ADVERBS
    Circle the correct word:

4. This red sweater will look (good, well) with black pants.

SIMPLE/COMPOUND/COMPLEX SENTENCES:
    A compound sentence is made up of two (or more) complete thoughts.
    These thoughts could stand alone as separate sentences.
    The coordinating conjunctions, *and, but,* and *or* are usually used
    to join the parts of a compound sentence.
        Examples: This bucket is heavy, but I can carry it.
                   The answer is fifty, and Mira has that answer.

    Place a √ if the sentence is a compound sentence:

5. A. ___ Kurt closed his eyes, but he could not sleep.
    B. ___ Her grandmother grabbed her hand, squeezed it, and laughed.

SENTENCE COMBINING:

6. A cucumber is a vine-growing fruit with a green rind.
    A cucumber tree is a North American magnolia tree.

_____

_____

DAY 98

CAPITALIZATION:

1. take interstate 10 and then go south on seventh street to reach bank one ballpark.

PUNCTUATION:

2. Alecs sister in law yelled clearly loudly and enthusiastically during the boat race

PARTS OF SPEECH: VERBS
   Write the contraction:

3. A. she is - _____
   B. I am - _____
   C. was not - _____
   D. cannot - _____
   E. could not - _____
   F. you will - _____

PARTS OF SPEECH: ADJECTIVES/PRONOUNS
   Numbers may stand alone; they serve as pronouns.
      Example: **Five** were dressed in long gowns.
   Numbers may modify (go over to) a noun; then, they serve as adjectives.   Example: I saw **five** elk in the forest.   (five elk)
   Write P if the word serves as a pronoun; write A if the word serves as an adjective:

4. A. ____ Devi asked me to wait **ten** minutes for her.
   B. ____ There were **ten** in each box.

SPELLING:
   Write the correct spelling of these words:

5. A. impure + ity - _____
   B. nature + al - _____
   C. spray + ing - _____

SENTENCE COMBINING:

6. Sandor was rummaging through his grandfather's old trunk.
   He was looking for antique clothes for a play.

   _____

   _____

DAY 99

CAPITALIZATION:

1. the dead sea in the middle east is one of the world's saltiest lakes.

PUNCTUATION:

2. A teachers conference   said Dr Oxnard is being organized by Mrs D Tang

PARTS OF SPEECH: NOUNS
  Some nouns totally change when forming the plural. child - children
  Use a dictionary if you are uncertain.

  Write the plural:

3. A. foot - _____   B. ox - _____   C. medium - _____

PARTS OF SPEECH: ADVERBS
  Write the plural:

4. I never seem to have (no, any) quarters for the vending machine.

SPELLING:
  Remember: Words ending in vowel + vowel + consonant (VVC) do
              not usually change when adding a suffix.
                Example: reap + er = reaper
              Words ending in consonant + consonant + e
              usually drop the e when adding a suffix beginning with
              a vowel. Example: saddle + ed = saddled

  Write the correct spelling of these words:

5. A. trouble + ing - _____
   B. lean + ed - _____
   C. riddle + ed - _____

SENTENCE COMBINING:

6. A male African elephant may grow up to thirteen feet tall.
   A male Asian elephant may grow up to eleven feet tall.

_____

_____

DAY 100

CAPITALIZATION:

1. pedro said, "look at my new german shepherd named boo."

PUNCTUATION:

2. Aren by the way saves one fifth of his salary

PARTS OF SPEECH: ADJECTIVES/ADVERBS
Circle the correct answer:

3. That horse doesn't jump (good, well).

SYNONYMS/ANTONYMS/HOMONYMS:

**Homonyms are words that sound alike but are spelled differently.
Synonyms are words that have similar meanings.
Antonyms are words with opposite meanings.**

4. A. A synonym for annoyed is _____.
    B. A homonym for peddle is _____.
    C. An antomym for prohibit is _____.

ANALOGIES:
Circle the correct answer:

5. ointment : heal :: jack-in-the-box : _____
    (a) entertain   (b) clown   (c) toy   (d) child

SENTENCE COMBINING:

6. These tires are worn.
    These tires are dangerous.
    These tires are almost new.

    _____

    _____

DAY 101

CAPITALIZATION:

1. they ate chow mein, a chinese-american dish, at lotus restaurant.

PUNCTUATION:
If part of a sentence occurs after a city and country, place a comma also after the country.
  Example: Tim visited Oslo, Norway, during the summer.

2. Laylas grandparents traveled to Ensenada Mexico by bus

PARTS OF SPEECH: ADJECTIVES
A proper adjective is derived from a proper noun.
  Example: Proper Noun: Asia
        Proper Adjective: Asian

Write the proper adjective:

3. A. Canada - _____
 B. England - _____
 C. Mexico - _____

PARTS OF SPEECH: VERBS
Underline the subject once and the verb or verb phrase twice:

4. Marta and her mother drive to town each Saturday and shop at a local market.

ANALOGIES:
Circle the correct answer:

5. fragrant : unscented :: hostile : _____
 (a) friendly (b) serving (c) deserving (d) unsociable

SENTENCE COMBINING:

6. A camel's hair brush is used by artists.
 It is made of hair from squirrels' tails.

_____

_____

DAY 102

CAPITALIZATION:

1. they visited hog island which is in northern virginia and on the atlantic ocean.

PUNCTUATION:

2. The mens swim team hasnt practiced at the Y M C A for several years

WORDS:

Circle the correct word:

3. A. (Their, There, They're) reaction was surprising.
   B. The smaller puppy was barking, (to, too, two).
   C. (May, Can) I ask a question?

PARTS OF SPEECH: PRONOUNS

Possessive pronouns show ownership.
Possessive pronouns are: my, mine   our, ours   it, its
                               his   their, theirs   whose
                               her, hers   your, yours

Write an appropriate possessive pronoun:

4. Marsh and Miki told _____ friend about the wrestling tournament.

ANALOGIES:

Circle the correct answer:

5. cup : pint :: quart : _____
   (a) ounce   (b) liquid   (c) measurement   (d) gallon

SENTENCE COMBINING:

6. The baby is crying.
   The baby has a fever.
   The baby has an ear infection.

   _____

   _____

DAY 103

CAPITALIZATION:

1. "the populist party was formed to express american farmers' opinions," megan said.

PUNCTUATION:
 Use underlining or quotation marks:

2. A. Amusement Park   (title of a poem)
   B. All Summer in a Day   (name of a short story)
   C. The Tigger Movie   (title of a movie)

SENTENCE TYPES:
 Change this interrogative sentence to an imperative one:
   Will you hand me a wrench?

3. _____

PARTS OF SPEECH: VERBS
 Write the contraction:

4. A. they are - _____   D. I will - _____
   B. will not - _____   E. cannot - _____
   C. he would - _____   F. here is - _____

ANALOGIES:
 Circle the correct answer:

5. watt : brightness :: gram : _____
   (a) weight   (b) pound   (c) ounce   (d) measure

SENTENCE COMBINING:

6. This camping spot is quiet.
   It is secluded.
   Few people know about this camping spot.

_____

_____

DAY 104

CAPITALIZATION:

1. was jefferson davis elected the leader of the confederate states of america?

PUNCTUATION:

2.
                                                7771 Neese Road
                                                Woodstock GA 30188
                                                April 12 20--
Dear Andy
     Come join our fun filled day of balloon rides water games and a picnic We hope to see you soon
                                                Your friend
                                                Karen

SUBJECT/VERB:
Underline the subject once and the verb twice:

3. Lori tugged the bracelet's clasp and inserted the oval part.

PARTS OF SPEECH: NOUNS
An indirect object is the receiver of *some* direct objects. You can insert <u>to</u> or <u>for</u> mentally before an indirect object.
                          to   I.O.   D.O.
    Example: I gave / my father his gift.

Underline the subject once and the verb or verb phrase twice. Label the direct object - <u>D.O.</u> and the indirect object - <u>I.O.</u>:

4. Jacy sent Amy a funny card.

ANALOGIES:
Circle the correct answer:

5. part : component :: choice : _____
   (a) division   (b) wisdom   (c) option   (d) complication

SENTENCE COMBINING:

6. Someone had forgotten to turn off the water.
   Our yard flooded.

_____

_____

DAY 105

CAPITALIZATION:

1. the organization of american states met friday in a latin american country.

PUNCTUATION:

2. Eduardo Chavez M D is all of the nurses favorite doctor

PARTS OF SPEECH: VERBS
   Write *present, past,* or *future:*

3. A. _____ Your aunt will arrive in ten minutes.
   B. _____ They grow radishes in their garden.
   C. _____ The teacher smiled at the children.

SENTENCES/FRAGMENTS/RUN-ONS:
   Write S if the words form a sentence; write F for fragment if the words do not form a sentence:

4. A. _____ Their dad cooks chili on cold evenings.
   B. _____ A rabid fox had been reported.

ANALOGIES:
   Circle the correct answer:

5. rope : tether :: tweezers : _____
   (a) tease   (b) pull   (c) cut   (d) splinter

SENTENCE COMBINING:

6. Two brothers ate lunch at a pizzeria.
   Before that, they did chores.
   They ate lunch with their cousin.

_____

_____

DAY 106

CAPITALIZATION:

1.   9555 madison avenue
                                     new york, ny 10016   **(A)**
                                     july 13, 20--

    my dear cousin,   **(B)**

       did you know that the milky way galaxy is shaped like a spiral? we are studying it in science class.   **(C)**

                                     your friend,   **(D)**
                                     kino   **(E)**

PUNCTUATION:

2. Are carp trout and salmon considered bony fish   asked Mano

FRIENDLY LETTERS:
  Label the friendly letter parts in number 1:

3. A. _____   D. _____
    B. _____   E. _____
    C. _____

PARTS OF SPEECH: **INTERJECTIONS**
  Write a sentence; use an interjection:

4. _____

SIMPLE/COMPOUND/COMPLEX SENTENCES:
  A compound sentence is made up of two or more independent clauses; these could stand alone as separate sentences.
    Example: <u>You may go</u>, but <u>you must return by nine o'clock</u>.

  Place a √ if the sentence is a compound sentence:

5. A. ___ Lani closed the mystery book and laid it on the table by her bed.
    B. ___ The speaker lifted a bird, and the students watched intently.

SENTENCE COMBINING:

6. A hammerhead can refer to a type of shark.
   A hammerhead is also an African bird.

_____

_____

DAY 107

CAPITALIZATION:

1. on june 15, 1215, king john of england signed the magna carta.

PUNCTUATION:
   When two complete thoughts (independent clauses) are joined by a conjunction (*and, but, or*), they form a compound sentence.
   Place a comma before the conjunction.
      Example: Some people eat snails, <u>but</u> I don't like them.
                   independent clause   independent clause

2. You must eat your vegetables or you cant have pie or cake

SENTENCE TYPES:
   Write the sentence type:

3. A. _____ Do you like to paint?
   B. _____ Please repeat after me.
   C. _____ Their ceramic masks have been fired.

PARTS OF SPEECH: ADJECTIVES
   Circle the correct adjective:

4. That is the (sillier, silliest) joke I've ever heard!

ANALOGIES:
   Circle the correct answer:

5. food : famine :: rain : _____
   (a) flood   (b) hurricane   (c) drought   (d) whirlpool

SENTENCE COMBINING:

6. A beagle is a small hound.
   It has a smooth coat.
   It is often used as a hunting dog.

_____

_____

DAY 108

CAPITALIZATION:

1. was okefenoke swamp in northern florida named by seminole indians?

PUNCTUATION:
   Punctuate this outline:

2. I Wind storms
       A Hurricanes
       B Tornadoes
    II Snowstorms

PARTS OF SPEECH: CONJUNCTIONS
   Circle any coordinating conjunctions:

3. After the theater performance, many stopped at a cafe and ate a late dinner.

PARTS OF SPEECH: NOUNS
   Write C if the noun is common; write P if the noun is proper:

4. A. ____ HORSE   B. ____ PONY   C. ____ STALLION

ANALOGIES:
   Circle the correct answer:

5. lawyer : attorney :: preacher : _____
   (a) sermon   (b) minister   (c) church   (d) altar

SENTENCE COMBINING:

6. Marco and Kammi attended an estate sale.
   They bought a screen.
   The screen is Oriental.

   _____

   _____

DAY 109

CAPITALIZATION:

1. go west on dreyer lane to rodrick stone company, grandma.

PUNCTUATION:

2. Ms Stella Holuba lives in a small rustic cottage near Frederick Maryland

PARTS OF SPEECH: NOUNS
   Place a √ if the noun forms the plural by adding s:

3. A. ___ collie   C. ___ gash   E. ___ glint
   B. ___ surrey   D. ___ doily   F. ___ trolley

PHRASES/CLAUSES:
   Write P if words form a phrase; write C if the words form a clause:

4. A. _____ From the very beginning
   B. _____ When Igor began to walk

SPELLING:
   A word ending in consonant + vowel + e usually drops the final e when adding a suffix beginning with a vowel. The e is usually not dropped if a suffix beginning with a consonant is added.
   Examples: rescue + ing = rescuing
              toe + s = toes
   Write the correct spelling of these words:

5. A. persue + ing - _____

   B. tie + ed - _____

   C. shoe + less - _____

SENTENCE COMBINING:

6. This bracelet is silver.
   It has turquoise insets.
   It has scroll designs.

_____

_____

DAY 110

CAPITALIZATION:

1. in world religion class, janny learned that the christian faith is based on the teachings of jesus.

PUNCTUATION:
   Write the abbreviation:

2. A. gallon - _____   B. foot - _____   C. boulevard - _____

PARTS OF SPEECH: ADVERBS
   Circle any adverbs that tell *when* or *where*:

3. When it's cold, we often go somewhere for hot chocolate.

PARTS OF SPEECH: PRONOUNS
   Circle the correct pronoun:

4. The clerk handed (we, us) shoppers coupons for toys.

ANALOGIES:
   Circle the correct answer:

5. now : present :: ageless : _____
   (a) interrupted   (b) neutral   (c) ceasing   (d) eternal

SENTENCE COMBINING:

6. The toddlers played on the sandy beach.
   Their mother sat under an umbrella.
   Their mother read a magazine.

   _____

   _____

DAY 111

CAPITALIZATION:

1. are morgan horses and chickens raised at willow mill farm?

PUNCTUATION:

2. Youre without a doubt the teams best player exclaimed Ned

PARTS OF SPEECH: VERBS
   Circle the correct verb:

3. A. I may have (drove, driven) over a nail.
   B. One thirsty guest had (drunk, drank) most of the lemonade.

PREFIXES/ROOTS/SUFFIXES:

   Prefixes help to understand word meanings.
   Some prefixes are used to express numbers.
   quad - 4 (quadruplets [four babies])
   quint, pent - 5 (quintuplets [five babies])
   hex - 6 (hexagon [six-sided figure])
   oct - 8 (octagon [eight-sided figure])
   Write an appropriate prefix:

4. A. Their grandfather had _____ruple bi-pass heart surgery.
   B. An _____opus is a sea creature with eight tentacles.
   C. The _____agon is a five-sided government building near Washington, D. C.

ANALOGIES:
   Circle the correct answer:

5. express : say :: postpone : _____
   (a) send   (b) receive   (c) prepare   (d) delay

SENTENCE COMBINING:

6. Trifle is an English dessert.
   Trifle has sponge cake in it.
   Trifle also contains fruit and whipped cream.

   _____

   _____

DAY 112

CAPITALIZATION:

1. wave hill mansion overlooks the hudson river in new york's bronx*.
*name of a borough

PUNCTUATION:

2. Arent we appealing the decision Mr Bodnar   asked his client

PARTS OF SPEECH: PRONOUNS
   Reflexive pronouns are *myself, himself, herself, yourself, ourselves, themselves,* and *itself.*
      <u>Theirselves</u> and <u>hisself</u> are always incorrect.
   Write an appropriate pronoun:

3. I want to create a special card _____.

PARTS OF SPEECH: NOUNS
   An indirect object is the receiver of *some* direct objects. You can insert <u>to</u> or <u>for</u> mentally before an indirect object.
                         for   I.O.   D.O.
      Example: Grandpa baked / our mom a cherry pie as a love gift.
   Underline the subject once and the verb or verb phrase twice. Label the direct object - <u>D.O.</u> and the indirect object - <u>I.O.</u>:

4. Their son bought them an oak bookcase.

ANALOGIES:
   Circle the correct answer:

5. beat : rhythm :: concept : _____
    (a) concern   (b) lunacy   (c) advertising   (d) idea

SENTENCE COMBINING:

6. The coral snake is a small one.
    It is a poisonous one.
    It is related to the cobra.

    _____

    _____

DAY 113

CAPITALIZATION:

1. the lady bought a japanese rug at dazel company furniture with her eagle express credit card.

PUNCTUATION:

2. My mothers cousin came to visit from Dublin Ireland last fall

PARTS OF SPEECH: NOUNS

Place a √ by the correct possessive form:

3. A. ___ Dans' mother-in-law   B. ___ Dan's mother-in-law

DIRECT OBJECTS:

Underline the subject once and the verb or verb phrase twice. Label the direct object - **D.O.**

4. The company must have sent the wrong order to us.

SPELLING:

You learned that a one syllable word ending with consonant + vowel + consonant (CVC) usually doubles the final consonant when adding a suffix beginning with a vowel. Example: sip + ing = sipping

Words of two or more syllables ending in consonant + vowel + consonant (CVC) usually do not double the final consonant when adding a suffix.
    Examples: button + s = buttons   partner + ing = partnering

Write the correct spelling of these words:

5. A. fret + ing - _____
    B. holler + ed - _____
    C. hammer + ing - _____

SENTENCE COMBINING:

6. Lida is quiet and shy.
    Her best friend is shy and quiet, also.
    Her best friend's name is Jemima.

_____

_____

DAY 114

CAPITALIZATION:

1. from 476-1450 a. d., a period of european history called the middle ages occurred.

PUNCTUATION:
Punctuate the parts of a friendly letter.

2.   13 Bond Street
           London England
           May 20 20--
   Dear Madison
      Im sending the book entitled Angel Unaware
                       Love
                       Pam

PARTS OF SPEECH: INTERJECTIONS

3. Write an example of an interjection: _____

PARTS OF SPEECH: VERBS
Unscramble the twenty-three helping verbs:

4. od - _____   yma - _____   slahl - _____   aws - _____
   sode - _____   gmhit - _____   lwil - _____   ewre - _____
   ddi - _____   stum - _____   nca - _____   eb - _____
   sah - _____   slohud - _____   si - _____   gineb - _____
   veah - _____   ldouc - _____   ma - _____   nebe - _____
   adh - _____   doluw - _____   rea - _____

SPELLING:
Write the correct spelling of these words:

5. A. cantor + ing - _____
   B. scrub + ed - _____
   C. rapid + ly - _____

SENTENCE COMBINING:

6. A peanut is a legume.
   The peanut pod grows underground.

   _____

   _____

DAY 115

CAPITALIZATION:

Capitalize this friendly letter:

1.
                      73354 harrison street
                      topeka, ks 66603   **(A)**
                      november 2, 20--

   dear trevor,   **(B)**
     would you like to go to the pacific northwest with us?   **(C)**
                         my regards,   **(D)**
                         josh   **(E)**

PUNCTUATION:

2. I believe said Ramon that youre leaving at 3 15

FRIENDLY LETTER:

Label the parts of the friendly letter in #1:

3. A. _____   D. _____
    B. _____   E. _____
    C. _____

PARTS OF SPEECH: NOUNS

4. Nouns ending with ____, ____, ____, ____, and ____ add <u>es</u> to form the plural.

ANALOGIES:

Circle the correct answer:

5. impractical : realistic :: pleasant : _____
   (a) offensive   (b) foremost   (c) polite   (d) foreign

SENTENCE COMBINING:

6. Aleta's first reaction was panic.
   Aleta sat down and closed her eyes.

_____

_____

DAY 116

CAPITALIZATION:

1. i. books
       a. mysteries
           1. fiction
           2. nonfiction
       b. historical romances
   ii. magazines

PUNCTUATION:

2. The M C Kraft Co has moved to 33 Trellis Dr St Louis Missouri

PARTS OF SPEECH: PRONOUNS
Circle the correct pronoun:

3. The postcard from Chiko and (I, me) should have arrived last week.

PARTS OF SPEECH: NOUNS
Circle any nouns:

4. In March, Tessa and she are traveling to Boston by train.

ANALOGIES:
Circle the correct answer:

5. mollusk : clam :: reptile : _____
   (a) invertebrate   (b) spine   (c) alligator   (d) snail

SENTENCE COMBINING:

6. Sir Arthur Conan Doyle was an English physician and novelist. He wrote Sherlock Holmes stories.

_____

_____

DAY 117

CAPITALIZATION:

1. the jackson historical society held a sunday afternoon picnic at caledonia state park last may.

PUNCTUATION:

2. During John F Kennedys presidency many Americans joined the Peace Corp

PARTS OF SPEECH: ADVERBS
   Circle the correct adverb:

3. The beagle chewed the third bone (more noisily, most noisily).

WORDS:
   Circle the correct word:

4. A. She (don't, doesn't) need any help.
   B. Let me know when (your, you're) ready.

ANALOGIES:
   Circle the correct answer:

5. yard : distance :: degree : _____
   (a) temperature   (b) hot   (c) thermometer   (d) temperate

SENTENCE COMBINING:

6. Our picnic has been canceled.
   It has been canceled due to rain.
   It has been scheduled for next week.

   _____

   _____

DAY 118

CAPITALIZATION:

1. the phoenix suns* played at memorial coliseum for many years.
*name of a basketball team

PUNCTUATION:

2. Elizabeth asked Havent you been to Madrid Spain in the summer

PARTS OF SPEECH: NOUNS

Write <u>C</u> if the noun is concrete; write <u>A</u> if the noun is abstract:

3. A. _____ sword   B. _____ sorrow   C. _____ feeling

FRIENDLY LETTER ENVELOPES:

Write your return address:

4. _____

_____
_____
_____

D. J. Lewis
12 Kauai Beach Drive
Lihue, HI   96766

ANALOGIES:

Circle the correct answer:

5. quadrilateral : rectangle :: rock : _____
   (a) machete   (b) granite   (c) field   (d) balsa

SENTENCE COMBINING:

6. Abbie had her picture taken at a pillory.
   The pillory is located in historic Williamsburg, Virginia.

_____

_____

DAY 119

CAPITALIZATION:

1. last fall, judge wing visited lightner museum and a spanish fort in st. augustine.

PUNCTUATION:

2. Chessa and Don lived in Lake Tahoe Nevada for twenty one years

PREFIXES/ROOTS/SUFFIXES:

Sculpt is from the Latin root, scupere, meaning to carve.
Using this information, explain the word, *sculpture:*

3. _____

SENTENCE TYPES:

Write an interrogative sentence:

4. _____

ANALOGIES:

Circle the correct answer:

5. chilly : icy :: hungry : _____
   (a) food   (b) hunger   (c) starving   (d) refueling

SENTENCE COMBINING:

6. An oval ball is used in Rugby football.
   The ball may be passed or carried.
   It may also be dribbled with the feet.

   _____

   _____

DAY 120

CAPITALIZATION:

1. in biology class at a local high school, students learned about mendel's study.

PUNCTUATION:

2. Mr Cord her kindergarten teacher spoke at a volunteers luncheon

WORDS:

   Circle the correct word:

3. A. Someone gave (their, there, they're) mother some oranges.
   B. I have a (real, really) bad headache.
   C. (To, Too, Two) much sugar isn't healthy.
   D. We know that (their, there, they're) coming to the brunch.

PARTS OF SPEECH: VERBS

   Place a √ if the verb is regular:

4. A. ____ to loop   C. ____ to teach   E. ____ to send
   B. ____ to lose   D. ____ to preach   F. ____ to mend

ANALOGIES:

   Circle the correct answer:

5. quilt : warmth :: shield : _____
   (a) strike   (b) battle   (c) metal   (d) protection

SENTENCE COMBINING:

6. Mrs. Hanson inherited a car.
   It is a 1935 car.
   The car won't start.

   _____

   _____

DAY 121

CAPITALIZATION:

1. the federalist party was started by alexander hamilton in washington, d. c.

PUNCTUATION:

2.
                                    1 S Stratton Street
                                    Gettysburg PA   17325
                                    May 20 20--
Dear Gregg
     The boys wrestling team from our high school will compete next week in Durango Colorado
                                      Your friend
                                      Paco

PARTS OF SPEECH: ADJECTIVES/ADVERBS
Circle the correct word:

3. A. This math problem is (real, really) hard.
   B. Allison plays golf (well, good) for a beginner.

PARTS OF SPEECH: NOUNS
Circle any nouns:

4. The woman greeted us at the castle and gave a tour of its moat, dungeon, and tower.

ANALOGIES:

Analogies may express place relationships. Determine how the first two words are related. Then, find the answer that relates in the same way to the third word.

        Never : forever :: past : _____
     (a) future (b) yesterday (c) weekly (d) decidedly

Never is the opposite of *forever*. The *past* is opposite of the *future*.

Circle the correct answer:

5. dawn : sunrise :: dusk : _____
   (a) noon   (b) night   (c) daytime   (d) sunset

SENTENCE COMBINING:

6. Elba is a small Italian island in the Tyrrhenian Sea.
   It was the site of Napoleon's exile.

_____

_____

DAY 122

CAPITALIZATION:

1. has aunt nicole bought princess ice cream or birds and bears* at miracle market on tenth street?

*name of a magazine

PUNCTUATION:

2. Mr Gores silk flowered tie with tropical birds looked great with his three piece suit

SUBJECT/VERB:

With either/or and neither/nor, make the verb agree with the subject after or or nor.

Example: Neither Micah nor his sisters (eat, eats) spinach.

Underline the subject once; underline the verb twice:

3. Neither her dog nor her cats (like, likes) to travel in a car.

PARTS OF SPEECH: ADJECTIVES

Circle any descriptive adjectives:

4. We made enormous chocolate milkshakes and chicken sandwiches for lunch.

SIMPLE/COMPOUND/COMPLEX   SENTENCES:

Place a √ if the sentence is a compound sentence:

5. A. ____ On Saturdays, Seth usually hikes and explores for an hour.
   B. ____ Dakota motioned to the travelers, but they didn't respond.

SENTENCE COMBINING:

6. His grandfather was a soldier in World War II.
   His grandfather was part of the famous Normandy Invasion.

_____

_____

DAY 123

CAPITALIZATION:
Capitalize these titles:

1. A. "teen angel"
   B. "out of the wilderness"
   C. "the back page"

PUNCTUATION:

2. The book entitled Two Pennies for Parker was a short funny novel

PARTS OF SPEECH: VERBS
Write *present*, *past*, or *future*:

3. A. _____ Carlotta asks so many questions.
   B. _____ The gold ore sparkled in the sun.
   C. _____ Will you buy a microscope with your money?

DICTIONARY SKILLS: GUIDE WORDS
Place a √ if the word will appear on a page with the guide words: party - praise:

4. A. ___ panic   B. ___ porous   C. ___ pram   D. ___ pastel

ANALOGIES:
Circle the correct answer:

5. haiku : poetry :: bonsai : _____
   (a) plant   (b) wrestling   (c) Japan   (d) story

SENTENCE COMBINING:

6. Sarah is a journalist.
   She wrote an article about saving whales.
   The article won an award.

_____

_____

DAY 124

CAPITALIZATION:

1. a vicksburg parade honored those whose ancestors fought in the civil war.

PUNCTUATION:

2. The producer the director and the script writer discussed the movies length

PARTS OF SPEECH: ADJECTIVES/PRONOUNS

Indefinites such as *some, few, many,* and *any* may stand alone; they serve as pronouns.
   Example: **Some** were dressed in long gowns.
Indefinites such as *some, few, many,* and *any* may modify (go over to) a noun; then, they serve as adjectives.
   Example: **Some** ducklings swam on the lake.   (Some ducklings)

Write P if the word serves as a pronoun; write A if the word serves as an adjective:

3. A. ____ Do you want **some**?   B. ____ I would like **some** mashed potatoes.

DICTIONARY: ALPHABETIZING

Place these word in alphabetical order:

4. mercy   prance   noisy   nosy   notary   practice   merchant

SPELLING:

Write the correct spelling of these words:

5. A. can + ing - _____
   B. cane + ing - _____
   C. hibernate + ion - _____

SENTENCE COMBINING:

6. Pago Pago is a seaport.
   It is located on Tutuila Island.
   Tutuila Island is part of American Samoa.

_____

_____

DAY 125

CAPITALIZATION:

1. at alpine german restaurant, sauerbraten and austrian potato salad are served.

PUNCTUATION:
When two or more complete thoughts (independent clauses) are joined by a conjunction such as *and, but,* or *or*, they form a compound sentence. Place a comma before the conjunction.
Examples: They may drive very late, **or** they may get a motel room at dusk.
Rica sang, Marla played the guitair, **and** Pia whistled.

2. Her foot was badly sprained and she was taken to her doctors office

PARTS OF SPEECH: VERBS
Write the contraction:

3. A. are not - _____   D. where is - _____
   B. I will - _____   E. will not - _____
   C. would not - _____   F. we are - _____

PARTS OF SPEECH: ADJECTIVES/ADVERBS
Circle the correct word:

4. That candle smells (good, well).

SIMPLE/COMPOUND/COMPLEX SENTENCES:
Place a √ if the sentence is compound:

5. A. _____ Devi could't find canned frosting, but she made her own.
   B. _____ Aren listened carefully and wrote his name at the top of the paper.

SENTENCE COMBINING:

6. Ben Franklin was the peacemaker at the Constitutional Convention.
   Ben Franklin later became the first Postmaster General of the United States.

_____

_____

DAY 126

CAPITALIZATION:

1. the corporate lawyer visited the southern part of alabama and stayed in a hotel on the gulf of mexico.

PUNCTUATION:

2. Yes Dan they live at the base of those high snow covered peaks

PARTS OF SPEECH: PRONOUNS
Circle the correct word:

3. Tom finished the house painting (himself, hisself).

PREFIXES/ROOTS/SUFFIXES:
Ous is a suffix that means *possessing, full of, or characterized by.*
Using this information, explain the word, *glamorous:*

4. _____

SIMPLE/COMPOUND/COMPLEX SENTENCES:
Place a √ if the sentence is a simple sentence:

5. A. ____ The seasick man grasped the railing and nearly collapsed.
   B. ____ His hair was freshly washed, and he rubbed it with a towel.

SENTENCE COMBINING:

6. Some children are sledding.
   Some children are building a snowman.

_____

_____

DAY 127

CAPITALIZATION:

1. "have you," asked lars, "been to waterpocket canyon in utah?"

PUNCTUATION:
Punctuate the following:

2. A. Visions in Charcoal (a magazine article)
   B. A Butterfly for Parkie (a story)
   C. Air Force 1 (an airplane)

SUBJECT/VERB:
Underline the subject; circle the verb that agrees with the subject:

3. One of my friends (is, are) very funny.

PARTS OF SPEECH: NOUNS
Write the possessive:

4. an office shared by two ministers: _____

ANALOGIES:
Circle the correct answer:

5. appetizing : tempting :: arid : _____
   (a) deodorize   (b) dry   (c) inviting   (d) sharp

SENTENCE COMBINING:

6. Alicia's brother and sister ate all of the cookies.
   The cookies were chocolate chip.
   Alicia had just baked the cookies.

   _____

   _____

DAY 128

CAPITALIZATION:

1. is castle chillon on lake leman at the base of the swiss alps in europe?

PUNCTUATION:

2. Pippas name if Im correct was listed alphabetically as Swesey Pippa

SENTENCES/FRAGMENTS/RUN-ONS:

Write S if the words form a sentence; write F for fragment if the words do not form a sentence:

3. A. _____ Although the fire went out.
   B. _____ Those boat shoes should prevent slipping.

PARTS OF SPEECH: NOUNS

Nouns ending in o add s or es to form the plural. If you are not sure, use a dictionary. If the word should add *es*, the entry will list *pl. es*. Otherwise, add *s*.

Write the plural:

4. A. moo - _____   B. tomato - _____   C. ego - _____

ANALOGIES:

Circle the correct answer:

5. healthy : diseased :: trivial : _____
   (a) nervous   (b) forceful   (c) common   (d) crucial

SENTENCE COMBINING:

6. The house was designed by Ludwig Mies.
   It is located in Chicago.
   It is on steel piers.

_____

_____

DAY 129

CAPITALIZATION:

1. is mt. elbert the highest peak of colorado's sawatch mountains?

PUNCTUATION:
> **If two describing adjectives joined by a conjunction *(and, but, or)* begin a sentence, place a comma after them and before the subject.**
> Example: *Lost* and *hungry*, the <u>travelers</u> were happy to see a light.

2. Peppy and smiling several cheerleaders ran onto the stage

CLAUSES:

> **Write <u>IC</u> if the clause is independent; write <u>DC</u> if the clause is dependent:**

3. A. _____ Kevin laughed.

   B. _____ If you need anything.

SYNONYMS/ANTONYMS/HOMONYMS:

4. A. A synonym for elastic is _____.

   B. An antonym for elastic is _____.

ANALOGIES:

> **Circle the correct answer:**

5. inch : foot :: ounce : _____
   (a) centimeter   (b) pound   (c) ton   (d) kilogram

SENTENCE COMBINING:

6. The flying fox is a type of bat.
   It eats fruit.
   It lives in Africa.
   It also lives in Asia.
   It also lives in Australia.

_____

_____

DAY 130

CAPITALIZATION:

1. in science class, i learned that the okapi is an african animal similar to a giraffe.

PUNCTUATION:
   Use underlining or quotation marks:

2. A. Back from Mars (title of a poem)
   B. Camping Life (title of a magazine)
   C. Vertebrates (title of a chapter)

PARTS OF SPEECH: ADJECTIVES/ADVERBS
   Circle the correct word:

3. This baked apple smells (good, well).

PARTS OF SPEECH: NOUNS
   Write the possessive:

4. an inn owned by two brothers: _____

ANALOGIES:
   The second word of an analogy may describe the first or show a characteristic or feature of the first.
   Example: sandpaper : rough :: satin : _____
   (a) fabric   **(b) soft**   (c) gown   (d) blue

   Circle the correct answer:

5. elephant : immense :: chihuahua : _____
   (a) dog   (b) Mexico   (c) unusual   (d) diminutive

SENTENCE COMBINING:

6. William Henry Harrison was the ninth President of the United States. He was called Tippecanoe.

_____

_____

DAY 131

CAPITALIZATION:

1. "my aunt," said jo, "visited chester county and brandywine valley last spring."

PUNCTUATION:
   Two complete thoughts that are about the same topic can be joined with a semicolon (;).
      Example: Matt went to a movie; his sister went to a hockey game.

2. Mrs Uman makes baskets youll find them at craft shows at the M T A* building

*abbreviation for Medical Transportation Association

PARTS OF SPEECH: ADVERBS
   Circle any adverbs that tell *where* or *how*:

3. The chef carefully cut wedges into the tomato and placed tuna within.

PREFIXES/ROOTS/SUFFIXES:
   Prefixes: trans - across (**trans**atlantic)   micro - small (**micro**scope)
                   semi - half (**semi**permanent)   post - after, behind (**post**nasal)
   Write an appropriate prefix:

4. A. Bacteria are _____organisms.
   B. The child drew a _____circle in the sand.
   C. Jana signed her name to the letter and added P.S. for _____script.
   D. That company _____ports furniture.

SPELLING:

   Write the correct spelling of these words:

5. A. casual + ty - _____   C. care + ful - _____
   B. care + ing - _____   D. rare + ity - _____

SENTENCE COMBINING:

6. The boy tripped over a garden hose.
   The boy fell on a wooden walkway.
   The boy broke his arm.

_____

_____

DAY 132

CAPITALIZATION:

1. my father and i like the negro spiritual entitled "swing low, sweet chariot."

PUNCTUATION:

2. Dad needs the following flour one third cup of sugar and apples

PHRASES/CLAUSES:

Write **P** if words form a phrase; write **C** if the words form a clause:
Remember: A clause contains a subject and a verb.

3. A. _____ Because we are making pancakes
    B. _____ Before the early morning traffic report

PARTS OF SPEECH: ADJECTIVES

Write the proper adjective:

4. A. Alaska - _____
    B. Spain - _____
    C. Greece - _____

ANALOGIES:

Circle the correct answer:

5. landform : peninsula :: vehicle : _____
    (a) car   (b) speed   (c) brake   (d) dealer

SENTENCE COMBINING:

6. The children are laughing.
    They are watching a show.
    The show is a puppet one.

    _____

    _____

DAY 133

CAPITALIZATION:
  Capitalize this friendly letter:

1.
  12 north 56th street
  orange park, fl 32073
  june 2, 20--

  dear mrs. luna,
     my mother received the lifetime achievement award from a service club in raleigh, north carolina.
  sincerely,
  jolene

PUNCTUATION:
  Place a comma after an introductory participial phrase.
  Example: *Standing in line*, the child became restless.
  Prompted by his mother, the child shook hands with me.

2. Stuck in traffic the taxi driver looked for a faster quicker route

SUBJECT/VERB:
  Underline the subject once and the verb or verb phrase twice:

3. On Saturday morning, Frank, John, and I are going to the skating rink.

PARTS OF SPEECH: PREPOSITIONS
  Box any object of the preposition:

4. A shrill whistle sounded from a nearby building.

ANALOGIES:
  Circle the correct answer:

5. penny : dollar :: year : _____
   (a) dime   (b) month   (c) decade   (d) century

SENTENCE COMBINING:

6. A seahorse is a semitropical fish.
   It normally swims in an upright position.

_____

_____

DAY 134

CAPITALIZATION:

Capitalize this outline:

1. i. american life
   a. colonial times
   b. modern times
   ii. british life

PUNCTUATION:

2. No their grandparents twenty fifth anniversary wasnt celebrated on Dec 16 2000

DICTIONARY SKILLS: ALPHATBETIZING

Place these words in alphabetical order:

3. attic   deal   antic   cattle   deem   antler

PARTS OF SPEECH: VERBS

Circle the correct verb:

4. A. The runner has (stole, stolen) third base.
   B. Ice cubes had been (froze, frozen) in odd shapes.
   C. Have you ever (took, taken) a trip to Minnesota?
   D. He (seen, saw) a mouse run across the floor.
   E. Have you (ate, eaten) breakfast?

SPELLING:

Write the correct spelling of the word:

5. A. stir + ed - _____   C. sweet + ly - _____
   B. freeze + ing - _____   D. annoy + ed - _____

SENTENCE COMBINING:

6. The couple visited Oatlands Plantation.
   Oatlands Plantation is an 1803 mansion in the South.

_____

_____

DAY 135

CAPITALIZATION:

1. the artist, william chase, helped to found the society of painters in pastel.

PUNCTUATION:
   If two describing adjectives joined by a conjunction *(and, but, or)* begin a sentence, place a comma after them and before the subject.
   Example: *Weary* and *tired,* the woman closed her eyes.
2. Happy and excited the children loaded the bus

PARTS OF SPEECH: VERBS
   Underline the subject once and the verb or verb phrase twice:

3. Put your clothes into the washing machine.

SENTENCE TYPES:
   Write a declarative sentence:

4. _____

ANALOGIES:
   Circle the correct answer:

5. kangaroo : Australia :: penquin : _____
   (a) Arctic   (b) Antarctica   (c) Iceland   (d) Vinland

SENTENCE COMBINING:

6. The woman was upset.
   Her poodle was lost.
   She was searching the neighborhood for him.

_____

_____

DAY 136

CAPITALIZATION:

1. in june, the democratic party held a convention in new york city.

PUNCTUATION:

2. Our principal Tom Nast makes short snappy speeches

PARTS OF SPEECH: CONJUNCTIONS/INTERJECTIONS
  Circle any conjunctions; box any interjections:

3. Whoa! Slow down and tell me exactly what happened!

PARTS OF SPEECH: ADJECTIVES
  Circle the correct adjective:

4. That dome is the (more unusual, most unusual) home in our neighborhood.

ANALOGIES:
  Circle the correct answer:

5. dance : waltz :: tea : _____
   (a) coffee   (b) caffeine   (c) tannin   (d) herbal

SENTENCE COMBINING:

6. The kitchen floor needs to be washed.
   The kitchen floor is caked with mud.

   _____
   _____

DAY 137

CAPITALIZATION:

1. samuel chase was an american revolutionary leader who later served on the u. s. supreme court.

PUNCTUATION:

2. Mr Greene said Fifty five people attended our horse lovers picnic

PARTS OF SPEECH: NOUNS
Write an example of a proper noun:

3. _____

PREFIXES/ROOTS/SUFFIXES:
Toxicum **is a Latin root that relates to poison.**
Using this information, explain the word, *nontoxic:*

4. _____

SPELLING:
Write the correct spelling of these words:

5. A. erode + ing - _____
   B. flap + ed - _____
   C. discreet + ly - _____
   D. supply + ed - _____

SENTENCE COMBINING:

6. The Gulf Stream is a warm ocean current.
   It flows from the Gulf of Mexico.

_____

_____

DAY 138

CAPITALIZATION:

1. the french explorer la salle claimed the mississippi valley and named it louisiana after king louis XIV.

PUNCTUATION:

2. Juanitas sister visited her mother in law in Lisbon Portugal last spring

PARTS OF SPEECH: PRONOUNS
Circle the correct pronoun:

3. It was difficult for (we, us) participants to understand his oral directions.

SENTENCE TYPES:
Change this declarative sentence to an interrogative one:
Their mother let them go sledding in the afternoon.

4. _____

ANALOGIES:
Circle the correct answer:

5. pimple : pus :: volcano : _____
   (a) eruption   (b) island   (c) spew   (d) lava

SENTENCE COMBINING:

6. A ceramic cup is for sale.
   The cup is shaped like a rabbit.
   It is for sale in a Victorian shop.

   _____

   _____

DAY 139

CAPITALIZATION:

1.   22 green lake road
                                     st. george, utah 84790   **(A)**
                                       august 23, 20--

       dear deka,   **(B)**

PUNCTUATION:

2. Jason Dill our neighbor restores antique furniture

FRIENDLY LETTER:

Write the parts to the friendly letter in #1:

3. A. _____   B. _____

PARTS OF SPEECH: ADJECTIVES/PRONOUNS

This, that, those, and these may stand alone; they serve as pronouns.
            Example: **This** is a very strange situation.

This, that, those, and these may modify (go over to) a noun; then, they serve as adjectives.
            Example: **This** book is science fiction.   (This book)

Write P if the word serves as a pronoun; write A if the word serves as an adjective:

4. A. ____ **Those** are my favorites!

    B. ____ **Those** pigs make so much noise.

ANALOGIES:

Circle the correct answer:

5. mistake : error :: lesson : _____
    (a) decrease   (b) teacher   (c) school   (d) instruction

SENTENCE COMBINING:

6. Paisley is a colorful cloth pattern.
    Paisley is also a city in Scotland.

_____

_____

DAY 140

CAPITALIZATION:
Capitalize these lines from a poem entitled "Habits of a Hippopotamus" by Arthur Guiterman:

1. the hippopotamus is strong
   and huge of head and broad of bustle;

PUNCTUATION:
Write the abbreviation:

2. A. centimeter - _____   B. cup - _____   C. president - _____

PHRASES/CLAUSES:
Write P if words form a phrase; write C if the words form a clause:

3. A. _____ Dipping cookies into chocolate milk.
   B. _____ The toddler helps to make beds.

PARTS OF SPEECH: NOUNS
Write the possessive:

4. Arabian horses owned by several ladies: _____

SPELLING:
Write the correct spelling of these words:

5. A. delay + ing - _____   C. star + ing - _____
   B. adore + able - _____   D. taste + less - _____

SENTENCE COMBINING:

6. Haleakala National Park is on Maui.
   Maui is an island of Hawaii.
   A dormant volcano is there.

   _____
   _____

DAY 141

CAPITALIZATION:

1. when nick had chicken pox, his cousin and i sent him castaway's* cookies.

*brand name

PUNCTUATION:
Two complete thoughts that are about the same topic can be joined with a semicolon (;).
   Example: Dinner is nearly ready; we need to set the table.

2. The cabin in the pines is isolated well need to take supplies

SUBJECT/VERB:
With either/or and neither/nor, make the verb agree with the subject after *or* or *nor*.
   Example: Either my mother *or* my aunts (is, are) making lunch.

Underline the subject once; underline the verb twice:

3. Neither the driver nor the passenger (was, were) hurt in the accident.

PARTS OF SPEECH: ADVERBS
Circle any adverbs:

4. She stepped aside, took my hand reluctantly, and suddenly fell down.

ANALOGIES:
Circle the correct answer:

5. forceps : grasp :: mallet : _____
   (a) pound   (b) pour   (c) trowel   (d) pallet

SENTENCE COMBINING:

6. An echidna is a spine-covered mammal.
   It is toothless.
   It eats ants with its sticky tongue.

_____

_____

DAY 142

CAPITALIZATION:

1. the greek poet named homer is supposed to have written in 700 b. c.

PUNCTUATION:

2. Bought by a racer the car was low to the ground sleek and fast

DIRECT OBJECTS:
   Underline the subject once and the verb or verb phrase twice. Label the direct object - D.O.:

3. Have you seen my jacket anywhere?

PARTS OF SPEECH: NOUNS
   Write the possessive:

4. A. a dog belonging to one boy - _____
    B. a dog belonging to four boys - _____

SPELLING:
   A word ending with a single consonant + e usually makes the vowel before the consonant say its own name. A word ending with consonant + e usually drops the final e when adding a suffix beginning with a vowel.
      Example: debate + able = debatable
   However, if c or g occurs before the final e, the e is usually not dropped when adding the suffix, able.
      Example: replace + able = replaceable
   Write the correct spelling of these words:

5. A. consume + able - _____
    B. recharge + able - _____
    C. love + able - _____

SENTENCE COMBINING:

6. Haute couture is the designing of ladies' high fashion.
    Haute cuisine is the preparing of fine foods.

    _____

    _____

DAY 143

CAPITALIZATION:

1. is the canadian remembrance day in november similar to the american veteran's day?

PUNCTUATION:

2. Kala Jose and she participated in the last event a three legged race

PARTS OF SPEECH: ADVERBS
   Circle the correct word:

3. You never have time for (nobody, anybody).

FRIENDLY LETTER ENVELOPES:
   Write your return address. Address the envelope to Kim Tsosie who lives in Philadelphia, PA. The street adress is 11542 North Third Street. The zip code is 19106.

4. _____

   _____
   _____
   _____

                    _____
                    _____
                    _____
   _____

SPELLING:
   Write the correct spelling of these words:

5. A. relative + ly - _____
   B. negate + ive - _____
   C. place + ment - _____

SENTENCE COMBINING:

6. Joel receives an allowance.
   Joel earns extra money by mowing his neighbors' lawns.

   _____

   _____

DAY 144

CAPITALIZATION:

1. jill and jacy's new address is 23 justine drive, colorado springs, colorado.

PUNCTUATION:

2. After a very long introduction Carol Tang R N spoke at the nurses conference

PARTS OF SPEECH: VERBS
   Write the twenty-three helping verbs:

3. d_____   m_____   s_____   w_____
   d_____   m_____   w_____   w_____
   d_____   m_____   c_____   b_____
   h_____   sh_____   i_____   b_____
   h_____   co_____   a_____   b_____
   h_____   wo_____   a_____

PARTS OF SPEECH: NOUNS
   Circle any nouns:

4. The bravery of the young knight was noticed by the king of his country.

ANALOGIES:
   Circle the correct answer:

5. generous : greedy :: humble : _____
   (a) poor   (b) proud   (c) humility   (d) regal

SENTENCE COMBINING:

6. Their dog has a long, shaggy coat.
   Their dog has long ears.
   Their dog is a cocker spaniel.

_____

_____

DAY 145

CAPITALIZATION:

1. we visited the thomas point lighthouse on the chesapeake bay near annapolis.

PUNCTUATION:

2.
                                3 E King St
   (A)   Shippensburg PA 17257
                                Oct 23 20--

(B)   Dear Aren

(C)   Ive bought a home in Brussels Belgium   Lets get together to talk about it

                            (D)   Friends forever
                            (E)   Mary Rose

FRIENDLY LETTER:

Label the parts of the above friendly letter:

3. A. _____   D. _____
    B. _____   E. _____
    C. _____

PARTS OF SPEECH: NOUNS

4. An example of a concrete noun is _____.

ANALOGIES:

Circle the correct answer:

5. topic : subject :: height : _____
   (a) tall   (b) elevate   (c) altitude   (d) alleviate

SENTENCE COMBINING:

6. His parents went on a vacation.
    They went to Maine.
    They visited St. John Valley.
    It has many potato farms.

_____

_____

DAY 146

CAPITALIZATION:

1. this spring, clayton school students will travel on arctic airlines.

PUNCTUATION:
 Place a comma after an introductory participial phrase.
  Example: *Hurrying out of the rain,* I accidentally bumped into someone.
  Listed below appraisal, the house sold immediately.

2. Waiting for a shuttle bus the travelers eagerly discussed the groups plan for cooking out

SENTENCES/FRAGMENTS/RUN-ONS:
 Write S for sentence, F for fragment, and R-O for run-on:

3. A. _____ Left by the side of the road.
   B. _____ Jana stirred the soup, added some salt, and then added more, but she didn't think that the soup was flavorful so she added even more salt.

PARTS OF SPEECH: ADVERBS
 Circle the correct adverb:

4. At the city-wide competition, Anita threw the ball (farther, farthest).

ANALOGIES:
 Circle the correct answer:

5. fish : halibut :: decoration : _____
   (a) guest (b) party (c) festivity (d) garland

SENTENCE COMBINING:

6. A door slammed.
   His dog became frightened.
   His dog hid under the bed.

_____

_____

DAY 147

CAPITALIZATION:

1. at a rodeo celebration, a group called silver heels played a song entitled "my friend for life."

PUNCTUATION:

2. Standing in line the lady read a book called Herbal Cooking

PARTS OF SPEECH: PRONOUNS

3. The personal pronouns that can serve as the subject of a sentence are _____, _____, _____, _____, _____, _____, and _____.

PREFIXES/ROOTS/SUFFIXES:

Like is a suffix that means *similar to.*
Use *childlike* in a sentence*:*

4. _____

ANALOGIES:

Circle the correct answer:

5. dash : stampede :: ravine : _____
   (a) rain   (b) canyon   (c) desert   (d) butte

SENTENCE COMBINING:

6. The teenager opened the refrigerator.
   The teenager took out cold meat and mustard.
   The teenager also took out lettuce and tomatoes.

   _____

   _____

DAY 148

CAPITALIZATION:

1. last winter, the torres family went to an aspen ski lodge for thanksgiving.

PUNCTUATION:

2. The class of 99 held its reunion many couldnt attended

SYNONYMS/ANTONYMS/HOMONYMS:

3. A. A synonym for strategy is_____.
   B. An antonym for conceal is _____.

PARTS OF SPEECH: ADJECTIVES/ADVERBS:
   Circle the correct answer:

4. A. His new contact lenses don't work very (well, good).
   B. Is this a (real, really) scary show?

ANALOGIES:
   Circle the correct answer:

5. lawful : illegal :: humorous : _____
   (a) radical   (b) witty   (c) serious   (d) joke

SENTENCE COMBINING:

6. Lani made an ice cream float
   She poured root beer into a tall glass.
   She then added ice cream.
   It was vanilla ice cream.

   _____

   _____

DAY 149

CAPITALIZATION:
  Capitalize these lines of poetry by Robert Frost:

1. whose woods these are i think i know,
   his house is in the village though,

PUNCTUATION:

2. Did you Carlo become seasick due to the swirling choppy sea

PARTS OF SPEECH: VERBS
  Write the verb or verb phrase:

3. A. _____ A cougar (past of *to growl*).
   B. _____ The salesman (future of *to present*) an offer.
   C. _____ Mora (present of *to take*) her lunch to work.

PARTS OF SPEECH: ADJECTIVES
  Circle the correct adjective:

4. Cody is the (friendlier, friendliest) member of his family.

SIMPLE/COMPOUND SENTENCES:
  A compound sentence is composed of two or more independent clauses (complete thoughts).   Example: I like to skate, but I fall often.

  Write S if the sentence is simple; write C if the sentence is compound:

5. A. _____ Th porter smiled, but she didn't open the door for us.
   B. _____ We took our dogs for a walk and then made popcorn.

SENTENCE COMBINING:

6. Tessa will sell tickets for the medieval fair.
   Tessa cannot attend the fair.

   _____

   _____

DAY 150

CAPITALIZATION:

1. in world history class, i learned that president john f. kennedy started the peace corps, and many americans went to other countries to help.

PUNCTUATION:
Punctuate the following titles:

2. A. Good Morning to You   (title of a song)
    B. Wallace and Ladmo   (title of a television show)
    C. The ABC's of Hawaii   (title of a book)

PARTS OF SPEECH: ADJECTIVES/ADVERBS
Write **ADJ.** if the boldfaced word serves as an adjective; write **ADV.** if the boldfaced word serves as an adverb:

3. A. ____ They stood **nearby** while the tow truck driver checked their car.
    B. ____ A traveler stopped at a **nearby** farm house to ask for directions.

DICTIONARY SKILLS: GUIDE WORDS
Place a √ if the word will appear on a page with the guide words:
chess - chime:

4. A. ___ cheese   B. ___ chirp   C. ___ chimney   D. ___ chill

ANALOGIES:
Circle the correct answer:

5. refuge : haven :: ally : _____
    (a) opponent   (b) friend   (c) attendant   (d) supervisor

SENTENCE COMBINING:

6. A starfish has five arms arranged like the points of a star.
    A starflower is a white or pink five-petaled, star-shaped flower.

_____

_____

DAY 151

CAPITALIZATION:

1. hanover methodist church welcomed reverend ron boyd with a sunday brunch.

PUNCTUATION:
   Two independent clauses (complete thoughts) about the *same* subject can be joined by a semicolon (;):
   Example: Pam changed hair stylists; she now goes to Cute Cuts Salon.

2. Pippi did well on her algebra test shes been asked to tutor other students

PARTS OF SPEECH: VERBS
   Circle the correct verb:

3. A. Deka might have (ran, run) in the last race.
   B. His mother could have (teached, taught) him to drive.
   C. These glasses must have (broke, broken) in shipment.
   D. I have never (lain, laid) on a feather bed.
   E. The trainer has (thrown, threw) a treat to the dog.

PARTS OF SPEECH: ADJECTIVES
   Circle any descriptive adjectives:

4. A brass antique urn was sitting on a small, hand-carved, cherry table.

ANALOGIES:
   Circle the correct answer:

5. drill : bore :: vise : _____
   (a) advice   (b) pretend   (c) clamp   (d) screw

SENTENCE COMBINING:

6. Cape Horn is located at the tip of South America.
   It is known for its strong currents.
   It is also known for its stormy weather.

_____

_____

DAY 152

CAPITALIZATION:

Capitalize the following titles:

1. A. "home on the range"
   B. "as time goes by"
   C. "more is less"

PUNCTUATION:

2. Her name was listed in the commencement program as Ramos Misty S

PARTS OF SPEECH: NOUNS

Place a √ if the noun adds *s* to form the plural:

3. A. ___ flea   C. ___ logo   E. ___ branch   G. ___ wallaby
   B. ___ elk   D. ___ metal   F. ___ potato   H. ___ roof

PARTS OF SPEECH: VERBS

Write the contraction:

4. A. it is - _____   D. I would - _____
   B. do not - _____   E. might not - _____
   C. you have - _____ F. you are - _____

ANALOGIES:

Circle the correct answer:

5. likely : probably :: forlornly : _____
   (a) sadly   (b) possibly   (c) luckily   (d) continuously

SENTENCE COMBINING:

6. Trichinosis is a disease.
   Someone can get it from eating improperly cooked pork.

   _____

   _____

DAY 153

CAPITALIZATION:

1. "what do you know about the frog legs festival held in florida?" asked ria.

PUNCTUATION:
   Use underlining or quotation marks:

2. A. the ship, Kristina Regina
   B. a nursery rhyme, Hey Diddle Diddle
   C. a magazine article, Home Is Where the Art Is

PARTS OF SPEECH: NOUNS
   Underline the subject once and the verb or verb phrase twice. Label the direct object - D.O. and the indirect object - I.O.:

3. I must have given my brother the wrong baseball card.

PARTS OF SPEECH: ADJECTIVES/PRONOUNS
   Write P if the boldfaced word serves as a pronoun; write A if the boldfaced word serves as an adjective:

4. A. ____ **Several** heifers roamed the meadow.
   B. ____ The teacher received **several** boxes of chocolate.

SPELLING:
   Write the correct spelling of these words:

5. A. adventure + ous - _____
   B. sole + ly - _____
   C. stun + ing - _____
   D. purify + ed - _____

SENTENCE COMBINING:

6. The whelk is a large marine snail.
   It feeds on crabs.
   It also feeds on lobsters.

_____

_____

DAY 154

CAPITALIZATION:

1. did you attend the harney country carnival sponsored by volunteer firemen?

PUNCTUATION:

2. A womens club meeting was held at 1201 E Clay Street Richmond Virginia

PARTS OF SPEECH: PRONOUNS
Circle the correct word:

3. They chose to build the cabin (themselves, theirselves).

PARTS OF SPEECH: ADJECTIVES
Circle any adjectives:

4. Two frisky puppies and a gray hound played in the muddy, tree-lined meadow.

SIMPLE/COMPOUND SENTENCES:

5. Explain why this sentence is not a compound sentence.
   While Mrs. Smalley ate breakfast, she watched the stock report.

   _____

   _____

SENTENCE COMBINING:

6. Mr. Davis is a businessman.
   Mr. Davis ordered a briefcase and business cards.
   Mr. Davis ordered an answering machine.

   _____

   _____

DAY 155

CAPITALIZATION:

1. the governor asked, "is miss jordan new to the department of energy?"

PUNCTUATION:
   Use underlining or quotation marks:

2. A. In the Stoneworks   (title of a book)
   B. Good Morning, World   (name of a television show)
   C. Aging Kitties   (title of a newspaper article)

PARTS OF SPEECH: NOUNS
   Write the possessive:

3. A. toys belonging to Russ - _____
   B. cupcakes made by several brothers - _____

PREFIXES/ROOTS/SUFFIXES:
   There are five prefixes that are commonly used to express *not*: *un, il, in, non,* and *im.*
   Using each of the prefixes listed, write an appropriate prefix:

4. A. _____related   C. _____literate   E. _____coherent
   B. _____penetrable   D. _____toxic

ANALOGIES:
   Circle the correct answer:

5. cutlery : knife :: crime : _____
   (a) jail   (b) theft   (c) sheriff   (d) law

SENTENCE COMBINING:

6. A family reunion was held.
   Marco's aunt and uncle from Iowa attended.
   The reunion was held at South Mountain Fairgrounds.

_____

_____

DAY 156

CAPITALIZATION:

1. lulu said, "my father lives in the pacific northwest* near seattle."

*name of a region

PUNCTUATION:

2. Loni his brothers girlfriend will be arriving at 4 00 P M

PREFIXES/ROOTS/SUFFIXES:

3. A. Would a subcontractor be the main person in charge? _____
   B. Premedicate means to take medicine _____ receiving treatment.
   C. A dog that is black, tan, and white can be called a _____ color.

PARTS OF SPEECH: ADVERBS
Circle the correct answer:

4. We edited our stories (more carefully, most carefully) the third time.

ANALOGIES:
Circle the correct answer:

5. commercial : sell :: newscast : _____
   (a) buy   (b) inform   (c) persuade   (d) demand

SENTENCE COMBINING:

6. A dugong is a tropical mammal.
   It lives off the Indian Ocean.
   It feeds mostly on seaweed.

_____

_____

DAY 157

CAPITALIZATION:

1. in the united states congress, the house of representatives is based on population.

PUNCTUATION:

2. My first grandchild said Sen Smith proudly was born on Monday January 1 2001

PHRASES/CLAUSES:
   Write **P** if the words form a phrase; write **C** if the words form a clause:

3. A. _____ Although Thong doesn't like oysters.
    B. _____ The dog helped the shepherd with the lambs.

FRIENDLY LETTERS/ENVELOPES:
   Write your return address on this envelope:

4. _____
    _____
    _____
    _____

    _____

ANALOGIES:
   Circle the correct answer:

5. dense : sparse :: friendly : _____
    (a) hostile   (b) respected   (c) talkative   (d) amicable

SENTENCE COMBINING:

6. Hail pelted our vehicle.
    The hail was the size of marbles.
    We pulled off the road.

    _____

    _____

DAY 158

CAPITALIZATION:

1. did abraham lincoln write the emancipation proclamation during a stay at a cottage called anderson house?

PUNCTUATION:

2. Yes our canoe trip is Friday we want you to come Cole

SUBJECT/VERB:
Underline the subject once and the verb twice:

3. One of the boys leaned forward and grabbed my arm.

PARTS OF SPEECH: NOUNS
Write the possessive:

4. A. a craft show sponsored by a church - _____
   B. a basketball team for men - _____
   C. pastries made by chefs - _____

SPELLING:
Write the correct spelling of these words:

5. A. stripe + ed - _____   C. rely + ing - _____
   B. strip + ed - _____   D. rely + able - _____

SENTENCE COMBINING:

6. The house has been restored.
   It had been built in 1956.
   It is a ranch-style house.

   _____

   _____

DAY 159

CAPITALIZATION:

1. grandpa ngi read the article, "traveling during the winter," in traveler's digest magazine.

PUNCTUATION:

2. Jennifer will you go with me to Cody Wyoming sometime   asked Polly

SENTENCE TYPES:
   Write an imperative sentence:

3. _____

CLAUSES:
   Write **IC** if the clause is independent; write **DC** if the clause is dependent:

4. A. _____ Unless the gate is open.
   B. _____ The car rental was very cheap.

ANALOGIES:
   Circle the correct answer:

5. teeth : gum :: aorta : _____
   (a) ear   (b) lungs   (c) atrium   (d) heart

SENTENCE COMBINING:

6. The class voted.
   The class decided to take an essay test.
   Some students were perturbed.

   _____

   _____

DAY 160

CAPITALIZATION:

1. is hoover dam located on the colorado river in southern nevada?

PUNCTUATION:

2. His reply without a doubt surprised Randy his dad and his mother

PARTS OF SPEECH: PRONOUNS
Circle the correct pronoun:

3. During each summer, Ria and (him, he) go to Idaho for a month.

PARTS OF SPEECH: ADVERBS/ADJECTIVES
Circle the correct word:

4. He moved his hand so (quick, quickly) that I couldn't see what was in it.

ANALOGIES:
Circle the correct answer:

5. pride : lion :: gaggle : _____
   (a) goose   (b) rooster   (c) choker   (d) joke

SENTENCE COMBINING:

6. The gorilla is the largest and most powerful ape.
   It is native to African jungles.

   _____

   _____

DAY 161

CAPITALIZATION:

1. with jefferson's louisiana purchase, america expanded from the mississippi river to the rocky mountains.

PUNCTUATION:

2. After the Memorial Day parade were staying with you until 4 00 Trisha

PARTS OF SPEECH: ADVERBS
Circle any adverbs:

3. Juan answered so softly that I could not hear him well.

SENTENCES/FRAGMENTS/RUN-ONS:
Write S for sentence, F for fragment, and R-O for run-on:

4. A. _____ Because she had a cold for nearly three weeks.
   B. _____ Noah had hiked all day he was exhausted.
   C. _____ Jina stuck her tongue out and made a funny face at the camera.

ANALOGIES:
Circle the correct answer:

5. particularly : especially :: alertly : _____
   (a) attentively   (b) instantly   (c) sneakily   (d) dimly

SENTENCE COMBINING:

6. A bug scurried across the floor.
   It was an enormous black bug.
   Everyone left the room.

_____

_____

DAY 162

CAPITALIZATION:

1. her grandmother, a member of hill country club, does not participate in any halloween activities.

PUNCTUATION:
Punctuate this outline:

2. I Patterns
    A Geometric
    B Spiral
  II Blueprints

PARTS OF SPEECH: ADJECTIVES
Write the proper adjective:

3. A. Germany - _____
  B. Ireland - _____
  C. Europe - _____

PARTS OF SPEECH: CONJUNCTIONS
Write a sentence containing two conjunctions; circle them:

4. _____

ANALOGIES:
Circle the correct answer:

5. morsel : food :: shard : _____
  (a) card   (b) casserole   (c) pottery   (d) piece

SENTENCE COMBINING:

6. Our plans are to visit an art museum.
   We may visit a science museum instead.
   We will do this next Friday.

_____

_____

DAY 163

CAPITALIZATION:

1.
                                         2 n michigan ave
                      (A)   chicago il
                                         nov 29 20--

(B)   dear wes

             our family went to the museum of northern arizona
(C)   last summer   we learned that early indians of arizona
            had turkeys and dogs as domesticated animals
                              (D)   your cousin
                              (E)   rosa

PUNCTUATION:

2. Punctuate the above letter.

FRIENDLY LETTER:

Label the parts of the above friendly letter:

3. A. _____   D. _____
    B. _____   E. _____
    C. _____

PARTS OF SPEECH: INTERJECTIONS

Write a sentence containing an interjection:

4. _____

SPELLING:

Write the correct spelling of these words:

5. A. atrophy + ed - _____

    B. discern + ing - _____

    C. ease + ment - _____

SENTENCE COMBINING:

6. A koala is an Australian animal.
    It dwells in trees.
    It feeds exclusively on eucalyptus leaves and buds.

_____

_____

DAY 164

CAPITALIZATION:
Capitalize this outline:

1. I. plant cell
     A. nucleus
     B. chloroplasts
   II. animal cell

PUNCTUATION:

2. Pat Mahlan master of ceremonies handed Nicole Yassi D A the award

PARTS OF SPEECH: VERBS
Write the verb or verb phrase:

3. A. _____ Her reaction (past of *to surprise*) us.
   B. _____ Mike (present of *to live*) in a college apartment.
   C. _____ Their wedding (future of *to be*) tomorrow.

PREFIXES/ROOTS/SUFFIXES:
Vid **is a root that relates to sight.**
Write a word that uses *vid* as a base and explain it:

4. _____

ANALOGIES:
Circle the correct answer:

5. Africa : continent :: Florida : _____
   (a) tropics   (b) cape   (c) peninsula   (d) swamp

SENTENCE COMBINING:

6. Dr. Jones examined the patient.
   Dr. Jones wrote a prescription.
   The patient was a poodle.

   _____

   _____

DAY 165

CAPITALIZATION:

1. last week, mayor troon played the clarinet in our town's st. patrick's day parade.

PUNCTUATION:

2.
                                      12893 W Summit Hill Dr
                                      Knoxville TN 37902
                                      February 28 2001

    Dear Aleta
        Peter is now twenty five years old   Its hard to believe that
my talkative energetic toddler grew up so quickly
                                        Yours truly
                                        Marcy

PARTS OF SPEECH: **ADJECTIVES**

    Circle the correct adjective:

3. Their friend seemed (more frightened, most frightened) of the group.

SYNONYMS/ANTONYMS/HOMONYMS:

    Circle any synonyms for *clever*:

4. clever: (a) obstinate (b) senseless (c) foolish (d) shrewd

SPELLING:

Write the correct spelling of these words:

5. A. love + ly - _____   C. omit + ing - _____
    B. succeed + ed - _____   D. refuse + al - _____

SENTENCE COMBINING:

6. The pin is sterling.
    She inherited it from her grandmother.
    It has many tiny pearls around the edge.

_____

_____

DAY 166

CAPITALIZATION:

1. in october, we saw a painting by john singer sargent in the chicago museum of art.

PUNCTUATION:

2. Wow Lu has moved to 1 Easy Street Carefree Arizona and she has seen a scorpion

PARTS OF SPEECH: NOUNS
Write an example for each type of noun:

3. A. Common: _____
   B. Proper: _____
   C. Concrete: _____
   D. Abstract: _____

PARTS OF SPEECH: ADJECTIVES
Circle any adjectives:

4. That new model home has tall French doors and a granite kitchen counter.

ANALOGIES:
Circle the correct answer:

5. suggest : advise :: change : _____
   (a) modify   (b) rectify   (c) meditate   (d) crucify

SENTENCE COMBINING:

6. A redingote is a long coat.
   It opens down the front.
   It is full-skirted.

   _____

   _____

DAY 167

CAPITALIZATION:

1. the kalish family visited the chihuahuan desert in southeastern arizona.

PUNCTUATION:

2. Yes well go to Montezumas Castle my friend

SENTENCE TYPES:
Write an exclamatory sentence:

3. _____

DIRECT OBJECTS:
Underline the subject once and the verb or verb phrase twice. Label the direct object - **D.O.**:

4. During the silver anniversary party, Mrs. Lu hugged Rebecca and me.

SPELLING:
You have learned that words of two or more syllables ending in consonant-vowel-consonant (CVC) usually do not double the final consonant when adding a suffix. Example: banter + ed = bantered

Exception: A two-syllable word ending in consonant-vowel-consonant (CVC) usually doubles the final consonant when adding a suffix beginning with a VOWEL *if* the second syllable is accented.

Example: be gin´ + ing = beginning

Write the correct spelling of these words:

5. A. forget + ing - _____
   B. begin + er - _____
   C. forget + ful - _____

SENTENCE COMBINING:

6. After dinner, Molly always rinses the plates.
   Melissa and Scott put leftovers in the refrigerator.

_____

_____

DAY 168

CAPITALIZATION:

1. the communist party under vladimir lenin took control of russia in 1917.

PUNCTUATION:

2. Your souvenir the small wooden carving will be your mothers favorite gift

PARTS OF SPEECH: ADVERBS
   Place a √ if the sentence is correct:

3. A. ___ Ivan doesn't ever spend any time with us.
   B. ___ We scarcely have no time to play.

FRIENDLY LETTERS:
   Use your address to write the heading of a friendly letter:

4.   _____
                                             _____
                                             _____

   Dear Seth,

SPELLING:
   Write the correct spelling of these words:

5. A. excel + ent - _____
   B. saucy + ness - _____
   C. pity + ing - _____

SENTENCE COMBINING:

6. The hostess welcomed the guest.
   The hostess introduced the guest to others at the gathering.

   _____

   _____

DAY 169

CAPITALIZATION:

1. several of his jewish relatives traveled to jerusalem for passover*.

* a religious event

PUNCTUATION:

2. One fifth of the class must bring the following for the craft yarn pine cones buttons and paint

PARTS OF SPEECH: NOUNS
   Write the possessive:

3. A. pearls given to Tara - _____
   B. problems shared by many cities - _____
   C. an opinion expressed by two women - _____

DICTIONARY SKILLS: ALPHABETIZING
   Write these words in alphabetical order:

4. pride   pardon   quiet   prim   quake   pristine

ANALOGIES:
   Circle the correct answer:

5. wave : gesture :: tag : _____
   (a) price   (b) clothing   (c) label   (d) knot

SENTENCE COMBINING:

6. Mt. Vesuvius is a volcano on the Bay of Naples.
   Mt. Vesuvius erupted in 79 A.D.
   It destroyed Pompeii, Italy.

_____

_____

DAY 170

CAPITALIZATION:

1. a greek student read about richard I in a british history class.

PUNCTUATION:
   Write the abbreviation:

2. A.   kilometer - _____   B.   pound - _____   C.   ounce - _____

SUBJECT/VERB:
   With either/or and neither/nor, make the verb agree with the subject after *or* or *nor*.

   Example: Neither <u>Micah</u> *nor* his <u>sisters</u> (<u>like</u>, likes) spinach.

   Underline the subject once; underline the verb twice:

3. Either his grandparents or his father (volunteer, volunteers) at that shelter.

PARTS OF SPEECH: NOUNS

4. An example of an abstract noun is _____.

ANALOGIES:
   Circle the correct answer:

5. emancipate : free :: mutiny : _____
   (a) mutter   (b) assist   (c) muzzle   (d) rebel

SENTENCE COMBINING:

6. Dad makes pickled eggs.
   He cooks the eggs.
   He peels the cooled eggs.
   He places the eggs in beet juice.

   _____

   _____

DAY 171

CAPITALIZATION:
Capitalize these titles:

1. A. "a big mistake"
   B. "a look into the future"
   C. much ado about nothing

PUNCTUATION:

2. Tina said Youve heard of course that hes moving

PARTS OF SPEECH: VERBS
Underline the subject once and the verb phrase twice:

3. A. Kim could have (came, come) earlier to help.
   B. A balloon has (bursted, burst).
   C. I should have (knew, known) the answer.
   D. Has Josh (beaten, beat) your record?
   E. The new juror has been (sworn, swore) in.

PHRASES/CLAUSES:
Write P if words form a phrase; write C if the words form a clause:

4. A. _____ Having gone to the market.   B. _____ The fall craft show was a success.

SPELLING:
Write the correct spelling of these words:

5. A. disgrace + ful - _____   C. deny + al - _____
   B. recur + ing - _____   D. strap + ed - _____

SENTENCE COMBINING:

6. The leather saddle was invented 2,000 years ago.
   It was invented by Asian warriors.

   _____

   _____

DAY 172

CAPITALIZATION:

1. samuel champlain, a frenchman, was the founder of fort quebec in canada.

PUNCTUATION:

2.
                                        12507 N 67th St
                                        Scottsdale AZ 85254
                                        June 1 20--
Dear Mano
     We arrived at two oclock last Thursday May 7   Lets meet next week at my aunts house on Elkton Ridge
                                        Always
                                        Lanzo

DICTIONARY SKILLS: GUIDE WORDS

Place a √ if the word will appear on a page with the guide words: freight - fresh:

3. A. ___ frequent   B. ___ freezer   C. ___ French   D. ___ fretwork

PARTS OF SPEECH: ADVERBS

Circle the correct adverb:

4. The detective examined the sixth piece of evidence (more closely, most closely).

ANALOGIES:

Circle the correct answer:

5. rejoicing : mourning :: split : _____
   (a) regain   (b) banana   (c) sever   (d) fuse

SENTENCE COMBINING:

6. Silver balls hang on a Christmas tree.
   The tree is gigantic.
   The tree is in a department store.

_____

_____

DAY 173

CAPITALIZATION:

1. is triangle x ranch located in grand teton national park of jackson, wyoming?

PUNCTUATION:

2. Yes those ladies holiday plans most definitely must be considered

PREFIXES/ROOTS/SUFFIXES:
Ologist is a suffix that means an expert in a specific study.
Card is a root that relates to the heart.
Using this information, explain the word, *cardiologist*.

3. _____

PARTS OF SPEECH: NOUNS
Write the plural:

4. A. child - _____   E. centipede - _____
    B. cliff - _____   F. sheep - _____
    C. trophy - _____   G. mystery - _____
    D. pitch - _____   H. atlas - _____

ANALOGIES:
Circle the correct answer:

5. swarm : bees :: drove : _____
   (a) swans   (b) doves   (c) turkeys   (d) cattle

SENTENCE COMBINING:

6. Ten cheerleaders ran onto the football field.
   The cheerleaders waved their pompoms.
   The team ran behind them.

_____

_____

DAY 174

CAPITALIZATION:

1. are the hausa people who live in nigeria of the islamic faith?

PUNCTUATION:
Place a dash (the width of <u>M</u>) or parentheses ( ) to provide additional information.
Example: The photographer told us to stand still -- perfectly still.
The photographer told us to stand still (perfectly still).

2. Our Mexican food was hot   extremely hot

PARTS OF SPEECH: NOUNS
Place a √ by the correct possessive form:

3. A. ___ writers' conference   B. ___ mens' club
   ___ writer's conference   ___ men's club

FRIENDLY LETTER ENVELOPES:
Write your return address. Address the envelope to Lou Mariana who lives in Honolulu, Hawaii. The street address is 2 Moanalua Freeway. The zip code is 96819.

4. _____
   _____
   _____
   _____

                              _____
                              _____
                              _____
   _____

SPELLING:
Circle the correct spelling:

5. A. amusment   amusement   C. applied   applyed
   B. writen   written

SENTENCE COMBINING:

6. Craig's neighbors rode in the Chunnel.
   They went from London to Paris.
   They were on vacation.

   _____

   _____

DAY 175

CAPITALIZATION:

1. during world war I, many americans fought in europe on the allies' side.

PUNCTUATION:

2. Their television was too loud too loud for me

PARTS OF SPEECH: ADVERBS/ADJECTIVES
   Circle the correct answer:

3. A. Their father lay down because he didn't feel (well, good).
   B. Is this a (real, really) scary movie?

SENTENCE TYPES:
   Place end punctuation; write the sentence type:

4. A. Yes! You did it   _____
   B. May I have a glass of lemonade   _____
   C. She insisted on washing the dog herself   _____
   D. Tell me about your new fish   _____

ANALOGIES:
   Circle the correct answer:

5. company : employee :: congregation : _____
   (a) church   (b) gathering   (c) person   (d) hymnal

SENTENCE COMBINING:

6. Thomas Kuykendall is an artist.
   He is famous for his duck carvings.
   He begins each duck with a block of wood.

   _____

   _____

DAY 176

CAPITALIZATION:

1. located in northeast tanzania, mt. kilimanjaro is the highest peak in africa.

PUNCTUATION:

2. I think   said Debra that Hampton Virginia was started by Jamestown colonists

SYNONYMS/ANTONYMS/HOMONYMS:
Circle the antonym for *optional*:

3. optional: (a) voluntary   (b) elective   (c) compulsory   (d) unforced

FRIENDLY LETTERS/ENVELOPES:

4. The two lines that are the same in a heading of a friendly letter and in a return address of an envelope are the _____ and _____.

ANALOGIES:
Circle the correct answer:

5. lethal : deadly :: effervescent : _____
   (a) efficient   (b) effective   (c) fluid   (d) bubbly

SENTENCE COMBINING:

6. Jackson is a cat.
   He belongs to Parker.
   Jackson weighs over twenty pounds.
   Jackson has a gentle disposition.

   _____

   _____

DAY 177

CAPITALIZATION:

1. he always reads "the midnight ride of paul revere" on independence day.

PUNCTUATION:

2. This recipe I believe calls for self rising flour   said Sharon

PARTS OF SPEECH: NOUNS
   Circle any nouns:
3. Bonnie and I have little patience for gossip and other negative comments.

PREFIXES/ROOTS/SUFFIXES
   de, ab, dis - away from
   co, com - together
   sub - under, below
   Using the meaning of the prefix, explain each word:

4. A. absent - _____
   B. subzero - _____
   C. cooperate - _____

SPELLING:
   Write the correct spelling of the word:

5. A. precise + ion - _____
   B. rally + ed - _____
   C. expel + ed - _____
   D. rally + ing - _____

SENTENCE COMBINING:

6. Wessex is a former Anglo-Saxon kingdom.
   It is in Great Britain.
   It is the setting for Thomas Hardy's novels.

_____

_____

DAY 178

CAPITALIZATION:
Capitalize these lines of poetry by William Wordsworth:

1. the world is too much with us, late and soon,
   getting and spending, we lay waste our powers:

PUNCTUATION:

2. That picture said Tate was done by Norman Rockwell a famous American artist

PARTS OF SPEECH: VERBS
Underline the subject once and the verb phrase twice:

3. A. The waiter had (brang, brought) water with lemon.
   B. Mom has (went, gone) out to repair our fence.
   C. The child was (sitting, setting) on a rocking horse.
   D. Have you ever (drank, drunk) raspberry tea?
   E. I must have (ran, run) out of time.

PARTS OF SPEECH: ADJECTIVES
Circle the correct adjective:

4. Their second guess was (more reasonable, most reasonable) than their first.

ANALOGIES:
Circle the correct answer:

5. exact : precise :: rich : _____
   (a) fertile   (b) poor   (c) precarious   (d) futile

SENTENCE COMBINING:

6. The Volkswagen Beetle was built in the 1930's.
   It was built in Germany.
   The designer was Dr. Ferdinand Porsche.

_____

_____

DAY 179

CAPITALIZATION:

1. "this victorian needlepoint," said alicia, "is that of mary, queen of scots."

PUNCTUATION:
  Use underlining or quotation marks:

2. A. a movie, Poor Little Rich Girl
   B. a plane, Hawk Hunter
   C. an essay, Comparing Haiku with Other Poetry

PARTS OF SPEECH: PRONOUNS
  Circle the correct pronoun:

3. The mayor handed Allie and (me, I) our awards.

PARTS OF SPEECH: VERBS
  Write a sentence using the future tense:

4. _____

SIMPLE/COMPOUND SENTENCES:
  Write a compound sentence:

5. _____

SENTENCE COMBINING:

6. She once had frostbite on her toes.
   Her toes become cold quickly.

DAY 180

CAPITALIZATION:

1. on labor day, our family will stay in an orlando hotel and visit the regency center.

PUNCTUATION:

2. A mens reading group is forming its first meeting will be next Thursday June 1

PARTS OF SPEECH: NOUNS

   Underline the subject once and the verb or verb phrase twice. Label the direct object - D.O. and the indirect object - I.O.:

3. That vitamin company has sent my parents herbal tablets.

SENTENCES/FRAGMENTS/RUN-ONS:

   Write S for sentence, F for fragment, and R-O for run-on:

4. A. _____ Holly cut lettuce from her garden.
   B. _____ Drew bought a 1950's jukebox it was too large to go through the door.
   C. _____ Art and history rolled into one.

ANALOGIES:

   Circle the correct answer:

5. coat : parka :: cloud : _____
   (a) stratus   (b) atmosphere   (c) sky   (d) space

SENTENCE COMBINING:

6. Amphibians have lungs.
   Amphibians are cold-blooded.
   Amphibians have moist skin.
   The skin is hairless.

   _____

   _____

DAILY GRAMS: GUIDED REVIEW AIDING MASTERY SKILLS - GRADE 5
ANSWERS:

AMV/RA: Answers May Vary/Representative Answer(s)
Other sentence combinings are acceptable.

Day 1: 1. Is, Jane's, Anchorage, Alaska   2. Tammy's dad left at 1:30 in the afternoon.   3. Sharon, sofa, apartment   4. today, tomorrow   5. (c) peaceful   6. AMV/RA: The clay pot is filled with yellow tulips.

Day 2: 1. In, September, Mr., Mrs., Pino, Grand, Canyon   2. That plant is tall, leafy, and healthy.   3. We <u>laughed</u> ~~about the sore on my toe~~. ***Note: Easy Grammar** is recommended as a teaching text that uses the prepositional approach. See last page.*   4. AMV/RA: My shoe is white with black stripes.   5. **(b)** resides   6. AMV/RA: Kim's aunt who is a dentist lives in Virginia Beach. Kim's aunt, a dentist, lives in Virginia Beach. Kim's aunt is a dentist who lives in Virginia Beach.

Day 3: 1. Last, Saturday, Riverside, Park, Cherry, Lane   2. No, we can't follow you.   3. with us   4. fast   5. **(a)** late   6. AMV/RA: Their father and grandfather are salesmen. Both their father and grandfather are salesmen.

Day 4: 1. Is, Thomas, Jefferson's, Virginia   2. Their new address is 9400 N. Offenhauser Drive, Flagstaff, Arizona 86004.   3. <u>Dorita</u> has   4. A. **C** B. **C** C. **A**   5. A. framed   B. pricing   C. priceless   6. AMV/RA: His cousin plays third base on a baseball team. His cousin who is on a baseball team plays third base.

Day 5: 1. My, Wood's, Canyon, Lake   2. I need the following: raisins, peanuts, and coconut.   3. A. who's   B. haven't   C. we're   D. didn't   E. I'm   F. I've   4. Jim and I   5. A. using   B. useful   C. leased   6. AMV/RA: Maria called to her puppy and held out her arms. Calling to her puppy, Maria held out her arms. (*Easy Writing* teaches students how to write varied sentences. See back cover.)

Day 6: 1. On, Washington's, Birthday, I, Newport, Beach, California   2. Dear Anna, I'll meet you by the fountain. Pedro   3. here, there   4. manner, nerve, noodle, offer, onion, pioneer   5. **(c)** shallow   6. AMV/RA: Allie's brown curly hair has blonde streaks in it. Allie's curly hair is brown with blonde streaks.

Day 7: 1. Is, Pike's, Peak, Rocky, Mountains, United, States   2. Tara's wedding shower was held on December 31, 2000.   3. A. pail   B. scene   4. A. **C** B. **C** C. **P**   5. A. posted   B. harmless   C. boarding   6. AMV/RA: Aren is taking his mother to her favorite restaurant for her birthday.

Day 8: 1. Does, Mr., Ernesto, Lopez, Eagle, Express, Corporation

2. I. Snakes
    A. Rattlesnakes
    B. Cobras
  II. Lizards

3. A. **C** B. **P** C. **C** D. **P**   **4.** doesn't   **5.** (b) obstruct   **6.** AMV/RA: Magma is molten rock that forms below the earth's surface.

Day 9:   **1.** During, September, Matt, Park, Meadows, School   **2.** Capt. C. L. Linski lives in a two-story townhouse in Hollywood, California.   **3.** AMV/RA: Do you have any chewing gum?   **4.** A. <u>or</u>   B. <u>and</u>   C. <u>but</u>   **5.** (d) broad   **6.** AMV/RA: Sponges have neither tissue nor organs.   Sponges have no tissue or organs.

Day 10:   **1.** The, Rossen, House, Heritage, Square   **2.** Brian, will you make strawberry-filled pancakes for breakfast?   **3.** AMV/RA: Where are you going?   **4.** <u>speakers have presented</u>   **5.** (c) completely   **6.** AMV/RA: Leeches are worms that have suckers at both ends.

Day 11:   **1.** We, Zion, National, Park   **2.** "I'm buying a three-wheeled bike," said Nana.   **3.** AMV/RA: gray (squirrel), oak (tree)   **4.** A. do   B. does   C. did   D. has   E. have   F. had   G. may   H. might   I. must   **5.** A. digested   B. amusing   C. bravely   **6.** AMV/RA: The peach pie is flaky and moist.   The moist peach pie is flaky.

Day 12:   **1.** I, The, Ten, Commandments   **2.** Yes, he's fifty-two years old today.   **3.** AMV/RA: A. nonstop   B. illegible   C. indecisive   D. unkind   E. impossible   **4.** AMV/RA: he, she, we; them   **5.** (d) attack   **6.** AMV/RA: Jasmin made a pink flowered dress.   Jasmin made a pink dress that has flowers on it.

Day 13:   **1.** For, Christmas, New, England   **2.** Yikes! You're here already!   **3.** AMV/RA: A. and, or   B. and, or   **4.** A. May   B. Can   **5.** A. voting   B. paleness   **6.** AMV/RA: Micah is related to Quahana Parker, a great Comanche chief.

Day 14:   **1.** The, U., S., Articles, Confederation   **2.** A. mt.   B. in.   C. ave.   **3.** from Mr. Davis, for my mom   **4.** gone   **5.** (a) destroy   **6.** AMV/RA: The spine protects the spinal cord and forms the skeleton's backbone.   The spine not only protects the spinal cord but also forms the backbone of the skeleton.

Day 15:   **1.** Dear, Clint, Dr., Vendi, Saturday, Always, Lulu   **2.** We're staying until 5:30 P.M. on Sunday, April 1.   **3.** faster   **4.** A. should   B. would   C. could   D. shall   E. will   F. can   G. be   H. being   I. been   **5.** A. blazed   B. rehearsing   C. trumpet   **6.** AMV/RA: A rattlesnake which is venomous has a forked tongue. The fork-tongued rattlesnake is venomous.

Day 16:   **1.** Did, Betsy, Ross, American, Boston   **2.** A. <u>Homeward to America</u>   B. "Dexter McDwyer"   **3.** A thermometer is a device for measuring heat.   **4.** brother, van   **5.** A. braided   B. steamer   C. boiling   D. tearful   **6.** AMV/RA: Plants use sunlight, water, and carbon dioxide to make their food.

Day 17: **1.** We, Africa's, Victoria, Falls, March   **2.** Marta muttered, "Your feet are covered with mud."   **3.** A. _ B. √ C. _ D. √   **4.** A. √ B. √ C. _ D. _
5. A. clapped B. drabness   **6.** AMV/RA: Although the circus is coming to town, I cannot attend. The circus is coming to town, but I cannot attend. *(Note: This is a good place to discuss that a comma is needed before the conjunction if it joins two complete thoughts.)*

Day 18: **1.** Last, Dr., Mrs., J., R., Stone, Everglades, National, Park, Florida
2. Was the two o'clock bus, Ms. Dunfy, on time today?   **3.** sit   **4.** too   **5.** (c) hue   **6.** AMV/RA: Hang gliders use currents of hot, rising air called thermals to stay aloft.

Day 19: **1.** Did, Walter, Cronkite, Colonial, Broadcasting, System   **2.** Susan, did Mrs. Prince arrive for her appointment at 2:30?   **3.** chosen   **4.** A. **P**   B. **C**
5. (a) ruby   **6.** AMV/RA: Solids, liquids, and gases are types of matter. Types of matter include solids, liquids, and gases.

Day 20: **1.** On, April, Fools', Day, Mayor, Dougal, Bahama, Islands   **2.** Long, sharp hooks stuck out from Mira's fishing lure.   **3.** good, well   **4.** AMV/RA: Vision is the ability to see.   **5.** (c) canoe   **6.** AMV/RA: Ben will give his sister a gold necklace with three pearls.

Day 21: **1.** The, Aztec, Indians, Mexico, Cortez   **2.** No, his name wasn't listed as Romero, Roberto.   **3.** in the rain; O.P. = rain   **4.** A. Pat's truck   B. that town's mayor   **5.** A. bowler B. thinned C. senseless   **6.** AMV/RA: Supersonic jets can travel at Mach 1 or the speed of sound. Supersonic jets can travel at the speed of sound which is called Mach 1.

Day 22: **1.** The, Marzanno, Italian, Roma, Gardens   **2.** The weather, I believe, will be clear today.   **3.** A. flee   B. AMV/RA: pull   **4.** Her <u>jacket</u> and <u>mittens</u> <u>match</u>.   **5.** (d) tennis   **6.** AMV/RA: Because Jamilla wants to become a Broadway actress, she takes acting lessons. Jamilla takes acting lessons because she wants to become a Broadway actress.

Day 23: **1.** A, French, Louis, Bleriot, English, Channel   **2.** "Stop the car!" exclaimed Chan.   **3.** well   **4.** Yikes!   **5.** A. lovely B. pressure C. touring
6. AMV/RA: Although the platypus is a mammal, it lays eggs. The platypus is a mammal that lays eggs. The platypus, a mammal, lays eggs.

Day 24: **1.** Last, Grandpa, Paradise, Speedway, Alabama
2.   16329 Blackmore Lane
                                              Henderson, NV 89015
                                              June 20, 20--
         Dear Miss Sells,
3. A. 3) heading   B. 2) salutation   **4.** A. √ B. _ C. √   **5.** (b) distribute   **6.** AMV/RA: A baby's twenty primary teeth are also called milk teeth. A baby first gets twenty primary or milk teeth.

Day 25: **1.** Pisgah, National, Park, Blue, Ridge, Mountains, North, Carolina **2.** Bruce, Rick, and Nathan went to the Y.M.C.A. (or YMCA) to exercise. **3.** ~~During the summer,~~ Logan <u>worked</u> ~~at a dude ranch~~. **4.** A. AMV/RA: rash, rashes B. AMV/RA: box, boxes C. AMV/RA: miss, misses **5. (a)** dampen **6.** AMV/RA: Kami's mother writes children's books. Kami's mother is an author who writes children's books.

Day 26: **1.** William, L., Shoemaker, Kentucky, Derbies
2. Outing List:
    -bandages
    -bottled water
    -toothbrush
3. A. _ B. √ C. √ D. _   **4.** aside, up   **5.** A. scared B. freshly C. repairing   **6.** AMV/RA: Her brother who joined the U. S. Marine Corps is stationed at Camp Pendleton. Her brother joined the U. S. Marine Corps and is stationed at Camp Pendleton.

Day 27: **1.** The, Daltson, High, School, Columbus, Day   **2.** The Rev. D. G. Raineri visited patients at St. Mary's Hospital at 6 P. M.   **3.** <u>PT</u>   **4.** AMV/RA: colorful (rugs); bare (floor)   **5.** A. fashionable B. releasing C. pressed
6. AMV/RA: A butterwort is a plant that traps insects with the sap on its leaves. A butterwort, a plant, traps insects with the sap on its leaves.

Day 28: **1.** On, Thanksgiving, Miss, Bengall, I, Cobbler's, Inn   **2.** The pilot studied her flight plan, checked her watch, and boarded the plane.   **3.** AMV/RA: I; we   **4.** tighter   **5. (c)** industrious   **6.** AMV/RA: Pia and Tim live in the same apartment complex on Rainbow Avenue.

Day 29: **1.** A. Sequoia, Scout B. Cannons, Comstock C. The, Key, Zion
2. Their business address is 2193 Cold Creek Drive, Sandpoint, ID 83864.   **3.** A. <u>bi</u>cycle B. <u>tri</u>cycle. C. <u>uni</u>cycle D. <u>mono</u>logue.   **4.** A. **C** B. **P** C. **C**
5. (b) suspension   **6.** AMV/RA: Robins live in that nest located at the top of that maple tree.   The robins' nest is at the top of that maple tree.

Day 30: **1.** Her, Canada, English, French   **2.** A. <u>Air Bud</u> B. "It's Feeding Time"
3. A. <u>**PR**</u> B. <u>**PT**</u>   **4.** My friend and I   **5. (a)** mammal   **6.** AMV/RA: Whereas a small galaxy may contain about 100,000 stars, a large galaxy may contain 3,000 billion stars. A small galaxy may contain about 100,000 stars, but a large galaxy may contain 3,000 billion stars.

Day 31: **1.** At, Cost, Club, I, Parchy
2. Dear Alicia,
        My family and I left for Mexico City on Friday, January 19, 2001.
                                    Love,
                                    Toni
3. often, together   **4.** AMV/RA: deer   **5. (a)** cat   **6.** AMV/RA: Each body cell has fluid material called cytoplasm.   Each body cell has cytoplasm, a fluid material.

Day 32: 1. Did, Aunt, Susan, Friendship, Bible, Church   2. "The boys' bathroom is locked," said Jacy.   3. A. he's   B. we'll   C. weren't   D. you're   E. they've   F. I'll   4. A. <u>F</u>   B. <u>S</u>   5. (b) shoe   6. AMV/RA: The three-cornered pine cupboard has glass doors.   The three-cornered cupboard that has glass doors is pine.

Day 33: 1. Many, Mississippi, River, St., Louis, Missouri   2. Gov. Thon and her husband visited Hartford, Connecticutt.   3. A. √   B. _   C. √   D. _   E. _   F. _   4. core, crime, easy, grab, great, heart   5. (a) ship   6. AMV/RA: Her favorite food is chicken marinated in mustard sauce.   Chicken marinated in mustard sauce is her favorite food.

Day 34: 1. Jay, Schooner, Days, Blues, Festival, Rockland, Maine   2. No, I don't want milk, juice, or soda.   3. for Lani; obj. of prep. = Lani   4. A. <u>A</u>   B. <u>A</u>   C. <u>C</u>   5. (d) poem   6. AMV/RA: Maria hit the softball, ran to first base, and waved excitedly.   After Maria hit the softball, she ran to first base and waved excitedly.

Day 35: 1. Lida, Don't, South, African   2. Toby, do I add one-half cup of cream to this dessert?   3. A. √   B. √   C. _   4. hardest   5. (c) steer   6. Although this oven cleaner is effective, it is poisonous.   This oven cleaner is effective but poisonous.

Day 36: 1. Dear, Nikko, I'll, Thanks, Your, Ricky   2. Well, who's the company's new vice-president?   3. <u>Scissors</u>, <u>tape</u> <u>fell</u>   4. good, well   5. (a) hand   6. AMV/RA: Because it has rained for two days, Edroe Street is flooded.   Edroe Street is flooded because it has rained for two days.

Day 37:   1. The, Qin, Dynasty, China, B., C.
2.   I. Flowers
    A. Bulbs
      1. Daffodils
      2. Tulips
    B. Seedlings
  II. Shrubs
3. well   4. <u>Shannon</u> <u>raised</u>, <u>waved</u>   5. A. begging   B. butter   C. scarred   D. caption   6. AMV/RA: Before Luke bought groceries, he went to the bank.   After Luke went to the bank, he bought groceries.

Day 38: 1. Does, St., Basil's, Cathedral, Russia   2. Pictures of a writers' conference appeared in a two-page layout.   3. AMV/RA: in the direction of west   4. <u>roads</u> <u>were</u>   5. A. insurance   B. dropped   C. trusting   6. AMV/RA: These wrinkled pants need to be ironed.   Because these pants are wrinkled, they need to be ironed.

Day 39: 1. In, Molly, Ryan, Incas, Peru   2. Sparky, our new dog, is our family's first pet.   3. Bob, sister, beach, Texas.   4. A. ridden   B. flown   C. built   5. (d) restless   6. AMV/RA: When Jana's watercolor of a parrot won a prize, she was very happy.   Jana was very happy about winning a prize for her watercolor of a parrot.

Day 40:   **1.** The, Himalaya, Mountains, Asia   **2.** A. bldg.   B. pt.   C. tsp.   **3.** AMV/RA: An inscription refers to words written on a surface.   **4.** A. good   B. well   **5. (b)** extraordinary   **6.** AMV/RA: The Sahara, the world's largest desert, covers nearly one-third of Africa.   Covering nearly one-third of Africa, the Sahara is the world's largest desert.   The world's largest desert, the Sahara covers nearly one-third of Africa.

Day 41:
1. I. Clocks
     A. Mainspring
     B. Pendulum
  II. Watches
2. He's twenty-one and a diver from Bangor, Maine.   **3.** may   **4.** A. there   B. They're, their   **5. (c)** board   **6.** AMV/RA: In 1891, James Naismith created the game of basketball for the Y.M.C.A.

Day 42:   **1.** The, Battle, Yorktown, American, Revolution   **2.** Kenny asked, "Where's my red baseball cap?"   **3.** and, but   **4.** A. Tara Hill   B. city, state, and zip (or) Scottsdale, AZ 85267   **5. (a)** aroma   **6.** AMV/RA: After the boy emailed his friends, he went to meet them.   The boy emailed his friends and then met them.

Day 43:   **1.** Susan, Did, British, Rocket   **2.** This beef jerky, without a doubt, is the toughest I've ever eaten.   **3.** AMV/RA: me, her, him, them, us   **4.** A. Their   B. there   C. to   D. Can   **5. (b)** attractive   **6.** AMV/RA: Although his aunt is visiting from Detroit, she is only staying for two days.   His aunt is visiting from Detroit, but she is only staying two days.   His aunt who is visiting from Detroit is only staying two days.

Day 44:   **1.** My, Uncle, Darius, Savannah, River, South
2. Dear Mr. and Mrs. Bencze,
    Yes, you're invited to visit us in Santiago, Chile.
              Respectfully,
              Ria
3. A. greeting (salutation) B. body   C. closing   D. signature   **4.** A. wax**es**   B. prong**s**   C. lens**es**   B. rich**es**   **5. (b)** scoop   **6.** AMV/RA: Lake Baikal, the world's largest freshwater lake, is in Russia.   Lake Baikal in Russia is the world's largest freshwater lake.

Day 45:   **1.** Did, Dad, Chinese, East   **2.** Sasha lifted her long, well-toned arm to shoot the basketball.   **3.** A. <u>S</u> B. **F**   **4.** <u>rabbi, son visited</u>   **5. (d)** catch   **6.** AMV/RA: These large pears are juicy because they are ripe.   These large pears are juicy and ripe.

Day 46:   **1.** During, Middle, Ages, England   **2.** "Whoa! This ski lift is so high!" exclaimed Miss Dee.   **3.** suitcases <u>toppled</u>   **4.** A. √   B. _   C. _   D. √   **5. (c)** protect   **6.** AMV/RA: Mr. Hart became perturbed when he received another incorrect bill.   Having received another incorrect bill, Mr. Hart became perturbed.

Day 47:   1. His, Frequent, Traveler, Club, Atlantic, Airlines   2. Lena said, "My uncle lives in Naco, Mexico."   3. A. **A**   B. **S**   C. **H**   4. AMV/RA: A. mountain, creek, man   B. Mt. Fujiama, Marsh Creek, Jim   5. (b) measure   6. AMV/RA: The large, square raft is slightly deflated.

Day 48:   1. A, Hispanic, Fairmont, Parkway, Friday   2. Sal Rice, R. N., works at St. John's Hospital in Jackson, Mississippi.   3. A. <u>pre</u>heat   B. <u>pre</u>wash   C. <u>fore</u>warn   D. <u>fore</u>told   4. A. **P**   B. **C**   5. (c) carver   6. AMV/RA: The swinging monkey is making funny faces. The monkey is making funny faces as he is swinging.

Day 49:   1. Has, Mayor, Miller, Rotary, Club   2. Jay asked, "Who's Lisa's teacher?"   3. good   (*Easy Grammar* texts offers similar strategies. See back of book.)   4. happening each week   5. A. mapping   B. relished   C. refinement   6. AMV/RA: We planted daisies, petunias, and daffodils in our flower garden.

Day 50:   1. Is, Democratic, Party, Uncle, Don's   2. The baby took a bite of food, smiled, and spit it out.   3. loudly   4. A. **MV**   B. **HV**   C. **HV**   D. **MV**   5. A. slurping   B. captured   C. swimming   6. AMV/RA: Whereas most butterflies fly by day, most moths fly by night.   Although most butterflies fly by day, most moths fly by night.

Day 51:   1. The, Pebble, Shoe, Company, Royal, Street   2. This package is for Tate R. Trainer, the town's only doctor.   3. small (hat), woolen (hat), black (hair), curly (hair)   4. <u>people</u> <u>stopped</u> <u>watched</u>   5. A. lately   B. lining   C. skimmer   6. AMV/RA: A camel, a ruminant, chews its cud.   A camel is a ruminant or cud-chewing animal.

Day 52:   1. Is, Rockefeller, Center, Lincoln, Tunnel, Manhattan, New, York   2. "Take me with you," Kendra demanded.   3. restlessly, somewhere, later   4. A. he's   B. we'll   C. weren't   D. you're   E. they've   F. I'll   5. (b) hidden   6. AMV/RA: After Jason and Hope ran five miles, they were tired. Having run five miles, Jason and Hope were tired.

Day 53:   1. Have, Bow, Lake, New, Hampshire
2. Boat Rules: Do not go beyond chained area.
                          Hold on while moving around.
3. We   4. well   5. (a) sturdy   6. AMV/RA: Christina's sister is a waitress at a Mexican food restaurant.

Day 54:   1. Did, John, Adams, Declaration, Independence   2. I'll need the following snacks: crackers, apples, and sunflower seeds.   3. us   4. good   5. (b) suspicious   6. AMV/RA: Because Lance was happy with his grades, he threw his report card into the air.   Happy with his grades, Lance threw his report card into the air.

Day 55: **1.** The, New, Haven, German, Club, Labor, Day **2.** A. "Beautiful Brown Eyes" B. <u>Town Tribune</u> **3.** A. **PT** B. **FT** C. **PR** **4.** A. **P** B. **C** C. **C** **5.** **(d)** see **6.** AMV/RA: When Chandra lifted the garbage lid and saw a snake, she screamed. Lifting the garbage lid, Chandra saw a snake and screamed. Chandra lifted the garbage lid, saw a snake, and screamed.

Day 56: **1.** The, U., S., House, Representatives **2.** "Please take this to the teachers' workroom," said Miss Krupa. **3.** A. **P** B. **C** **4.** hotter **5.** **(d)** coin **6.** AMV/RA: Juan is rather quiet, but his brother is loud and boisterous. Although Juan is rather quiet, his brother is loud and boisterous.

Day 57: **1.** Take, Constitution, Avenue, Lincoln, Memorial, Washington, D., C. **2.** Is the girls' club located at 909 W. Van Riper Road, Montvale, NJ 07645? **3.** A. declarative B. interrogative C. imperative **4.** A. √ B. _ C. √ D. √ **5.** A. amazement B. rudely C. composing **6.** AMV/RA: Most volcanoes lie in a zone near the edge of the Pacific Ocean called "Ring of Fire." Most volcanoes lie in the "Ring of Fire," a zone near the edge of the Pacific Ocean.

Day 58: **1.** In, Sea, Fever, John, Masefield **2.** This pantry, we believe, needs to be stocked with the following: soup, rice, and tuna. **3.** A. **DC** B. **IC** **4.** better **5.** A. presenter B. meeting C. debator **6.** AMV/RA: Erosion can be caused by water, wind, or ice.

Day 59: **1.** When, I, Across **2.** Tony's sister lives at 2 Southwest 5th Street, Miami, FL 33135. **3.** AMV/RA: to carry or move from one place to another **4.** <u>tray</u>, <u>cake</u> <u>have been ordered</u> **5.** **(b)** spoke **6.** AMV/RA: Mother is trying to light the grill, but the charcoal won't ignite. Mother is trying to light the grill; however, the charcoal won't ignite.

Day 60: **1.** Is, Gypsum, Cave, Nelles, Air, Force, Base, Kyla **2.** Mrs. Orwig's name was listed on the commencement list as Orwig, Lali. **3.** A. 17257 B. Vargas **4.** doesn't **5.** **(c)** pounding **6.** AMV/RA: Linda wants to go with her friends to Alaska this summer.

Day 61: **1.** Did, Grandpa, U., S., S., Constitution, Boston
2.
                         12235 Pleasant Street
                         Salem, MA 01970
                         January 27, 20--
Dear Cal,
      Our new rug has an unusual design and is woven.
                         Your uncle,
                         Rafe

3. A. greeting (salutation) B. closing **4.** bass, bath, earn, forest, jade, jail, jar **5.** AMV/RA: His brother is a wrestler. **6.** AMV/RA: When Joy went to the pharmacy, her prescription was not ready.

Day 62: 1. Salton, Sea, California's, Chocolate, Mountains   2. Mario asked, "Where's Parker's picture?"   3. A. real B. really   4. A. given B. fallen   5. A. studied B. studying C. studies   6. AMV/RA: Eyeballs are protected by bony structures called orbits.   Bony structures called orbits protect eyeballs.

Day 63:
1.   I. Mineral resources
     A. Oil
     B. Coal
  II. Other resources
2. Jana asked, "Aren't your parents from Finland, Kami?"   3. A. √ B. √ C. _ D. √   4. AMV/RA: me, him, her, them, us   5. A. relied B. relying C. frying   6. AMV/RA: The mother is ignoring her screaming toddler who doesn't want to take a nap. Although the toddler who doesn't want to nap is screaming, his mother is ignoring him.

Day 64:   1. North, Perry, Drive, Fort, Worth, TX, November, Dear, Anne   2. Yes, my mother or my aunt will present a slide show on Tuesday, Feb. 12.   3. A. **C** B. **A** C. **A**   4. A. **S** B. **F**   5. (c) lenient   6. AMV/RA: Mark wore a pink silk tie with a black suit to his cousin's wedding. When attending his cousin's wedding, Mark wore a pink silk tie and a black suit.

Day 65:   1. A. The, Fence, Post   B. Colorado, History, Kids   C. She, Walks, Beauty
2.   I. Snakes
     A. Rattlesnakes
     B. Cobras
  II. Lizards
3. AMV/RA: very, so, rather   4. that family's pet   5. (c) four   6. AMV/RA: This yellow musical giraffe belongs to a baby.

Day 66: 1. The, African, Professor, Shand   2. Yes, Allen, we're leaving for Hyattsville at two o'clock this afternoon.   3. A. √ B. √ C. √ D. _ E. √ F. √ G. √ H. _ I. √   4. team <u>is</u>   5. (c) pennant   6. AMV/RA: When lightning struck the tree, it split at its base. Because lightning struck the tree, it split at its base.

Day 67:   1. Did, King, Henry, England, Mary, Rose   2. Jordan's family rode on an outrigger, a type of canoe used on the ocean.   3. A. submerged B. reverse C. hypersensitive D. proceed   4. floats, parade, park, statue   5. (c) authentic   6. AMV/RA: Maria's mother likes opera, but her father doesn't. Although Maria likes opera, her father doesn't.

Day 68:
1. The rain to the wind said,
   "You push and I'll pelt."
2. "Yes, I'd love a strawberry-filled ice cream cone," declared Mona.   3. A. lying B. bought C. shaken   4. A. Can B. they're C. two, too   5. (b) nomad   6.

AMV/RA: The surprised girl placed her hand over her mouth and giggled.   As the surprised girl placed her hand over her mouth, she giggled. The girl who was surprised placed her hand over her mouth and giggled.

Day 69:   **1.** We, Galveston, Texas, Gulf, Mexico   **2.** After the baby's christening, the family gathered at the sister-in-law's home for lunch.   **3.** AMV/RA: She likes to row, **but** she dislikes sailing. (**and**, **or**)   **4.** quickly, carefully   **5.** AMV/RA: A. When I was five years old, I learned to ride a bike.   B. After we watched a movie, we ate a snack.   **6.** AMV/RA: Venus, the second planet from the sun, is a rocky planet. The rocky planet of Venus is the second planet from the sun.

Day 70:
1. I. Types of apartments
    A. Furnished
    B. Unfurnished
  II. Types of houses
2. A. U. S.   B. m   C. qt.   **3.** her   **4.** A. <u>C</u>   B. <u>P</u>   **5.** (c) wolf   **6.** AMV/RA: A small blue jay with a twig in its beak hopped around the patio. Hopping around the patio, a small blue jay had a twig in its beak.

Day 71:   **1.** Let's, Woodbury, Mall, Chippenham, Parkway, Richmond   **2.** The winner, by the way, hasn't been decided, Noah.   **3.** A. <u>IC</u>   B. <u>DC</u>   **4.** speaks   **5.** (d) New Mexico   **6.** AMV/RA: Jina's head hurts because she bumped it on the car door. Having bumped her head on a car door, Jina's head hurts.

Day 72:   **1.** Is, Jones, Bay, Croatan, National, Forest, North, Carolina   **2.** Their grandparents' anniversary, I assume, is next Wednesday, July 7.   **3.** A. not B. so C. too D. very E. rather F. somewhat G. quite   **4.** (You) <u>Wait</u>   **5.** (d) ram   **6.** AMV/RA: After they drove on Interstate 70 for ten miles, they took a county road to a cabin.

Day 73:   **1.** Yesterday, Beth's, Southwest, German   **2.** He did it purposely – to prove a point. *or* (to prove a point)   **3.** A. √ B. √ C. √ D. _   **4.** <u>police</u>, <u>crews helped</u>   **5.** (b) actress   **6.** AMV/RA: American football is played with eleven players; Canadian football is played with twelve players. Whereas American football is played with eleven players, Canadian football is played with twelve players.

Day 74:   **1.** Governor, Brinwood, Republican, Gooseberry, Inn   **2.** Their new son, I think, is being dedicated on Sunday, April 30.   **3.** <u>child</u> <u>took</u>, <u>crossed</u>   **4.** good   **5.** A. laziness B. merriment C. icily   **6.** AMV/RA: After treasure maps were handed out, the children began to search for a metal box. Treasure maps were handed out, and the children began to search for a metal box.

Day 75:   **1.** A, Polynesian, Hawaiian, Luau, Restaurant   **2.** Angelo exclaimed, "Wow! What a view!"   **3.** A. doesn't B. there's C. they're D. won't E. I've F. shouldn't   **4.** well   **5.** A. compliance B. steadily C. crying   **6.** AMV/RA: Jim found a soda can, several coins, and a child's shovel with his new metal detector. When Jim used his new metal detector, he found a soda can, several coins, and a child's shovel.

Day 76:   1. During, Space, Age, Neil, Armstrong   2. Both of his sisters' employer is Noah B. Troon, D.D.S.   3. Plush (bears), musical (bears), soft (sofa), leather (sofa)   4. A. **S** B. **H** C. **A**   5. (b) unlike   6. AMV/RA: Because his skin is very fair, he burns easily. His fair skin causes him to burn easily.

Day 77:   1. The, Wales, Alaska, Bering, Strait   2. A. Boating B. "Healthy Eating Habits" C. Other Skies   3. A. √ B. _   4. the act of finishing   5. A. destroying B. payment C. replayed   6. AMV/RA: The grandmother who bathed the baby laughed at the baby's silly faces. During the baby's bath, the grandmother laughed at the baby's silly faces. As the grandmother bathed the baby, she laughed at his silly faces.

Day 78:   1. Did, Michelangelo, The, Rebel, Slave   2. At the end of the month, Julie's mom always balances her checkbook.   3. A. **FT** B. **PR** C. **PT**   4. oldest   5. A. obeyed B. silliness C. boyish   6. AMV/RA: Patty's large blue eyes are very expressive. Patty's blue eyes are large and very expressive.

Day 79:   1. Banyan, Trail, Boca, Raton, FL, October, Dear, Aunt, Sharon, Have, Your, Mike   2. David can't go with us because his brother-in-law is visiting from Dayton, Ohio.   3. A. heading B. greeting or salutation C. body D. closing E. signature   4. ~~On a very clear night~~, we looked ~~at the moon through our telescope~~.   5. A. responsive B. lacy C. prettily   6. AMV/RA: Tara is a volunteer candy striper several hours a week at a local hospital. Tara is a candy striper who volunteers several hours a week at a local hospital.

Day 80:   1. Is, Islamic, Moslem
2. Dear Jemima,
        You asked about Nick and Anne's wedding. They
    were married on Sunday, December 24, 2000.
                              Trena
3. A. **C** B. **C** C. **P**   4. on the table, obj. of prep. = table; by the front door, obj. of the prep. = door   5. (a) heat   6. AMV/RA: The trireme, a type of ship used in 400 A. D., was powered by 170 oarsmen. The trireme which was a type of ship used in 400 A. D. was powered by 170 oarsmen. (**Note:** In the second sentence, the question may arise concerning the placement of commas before and after the clause, *which was a type of ship used in 400 A. D.* The rule is that commas are not used if the clause is essential to the meaning of the sentence. Because the fact that a trireme is a type of ship is included within the clause and, thus, essential to the sentence, commas have not been used.)

Day 81:   1. The, Magellan, Cape, Horn, South, America.   2. I've always wanted to go to Kansas City, Missouri, to see my cousins.   3. rather, not, very   4. A. you'll B. I'd C. weren't D. what's E. I'm F. you're   5. (c) destruction   6. AMV/RA: As the wind blew strongly, waves smashed against the rocks. The wind blew strongly, and waves smashed against the rocks.

Day 82: 1. A. Ultimate, Visual, Dictionary B. In, Early, Morning C. Autos, Their, Owners   2. Prepared for the worst, Mona marched into her supervisor's office.   3. AMV/RA: her   4. A. exclamatory B. imperative C. interrogative   5. (c) movement   6. AMV/RA: The moon, the Earth's only natural satellite, takes 27.3 days to rotate around the Earth. The moon, which is the Earth's only natural satellite, takes 27.3 days to rotate around the Earth.

Day 83: 1. Were, German, World, War
2.
                    Post Office Box 25022
                    Madison, WI 53701
                    March 4, 20--
Dear Joy,
      Matt, Chrissy, and I bought a new horse last night.
                    Your niece,
                    Lucy
3. we   4. Stop that.   5. A. demanding B. coiling C. rustic   6. AMV/RA: The model whose smile dazzles everyone has shiny white teeth. The model has shiny white teeth, and her smile dazzles everyone. The model who has shiny white teeth has a smile that dazzles everyone.

Day 84: 1. The, British, Sir, Joseph, Paxton, London's, Crystal, Palace   2. Can koi, a type of tropical fish, live to be over two hundred years old?   3. A. brought B. written C. swum   4. A. **DC** B. **IC**   5. A. flashing B. paddled C. bubbling   6. AMV/RA: Alana is a photographer who specializes in children's portraits. Alana, a photographer, specializes in children's portraits.

Day 85: 1. During, Revolutionary, War, Samuel, Adams, Boston, Tea, Party
2. Haven't you ever met these triplets: (or ,) Nick, Nicole, and Nina?   3. Grandmother's quilt   4. AMV/RA: with a horse, horseback riding   5. A. babied B. babying C. strapping   6. AMV/RA: The rain ceased in the early morning, and the sun shone for the rest of the day. After the rain ceased in the early morning, the sun shone for the rest of the day.

Day 86: 1. The, Henry, Wadsworth, Longfellow, Bowdoin, College, Maine.
2. "Well, these rocks, of course, aren't valuable," said Cam mildly.   3. pasta, paste, range, stare, story, track   4. worker <u>sold</u> D.O.= stamp, I. O.= me   5. (d) husband
6. AMV/RA: Ellis Island which is in the harbor of New York was once an examination center for immigrants to America. Located in the harbor of New York, Ellis Island was once an examination center for immigrants to America. Ellis Island in New York harbor was once the an examination center for immigrants to America.

Day 87: 1. Having, Nordic, Medical, Center, February   2. "I've mentioned that you're not pleased with their decision," said Mrs. Korte.   3. Intj. = Whew!; Conj. = but, or   4. A. **F** B. **S**   5. (a) purify   6. AMV/RA: Angling means fishing with a rod, reel, line, or a lure. Angling means fishing with the following items: rod, reel, line, and lure.

Day 88: 1. On, Valentine's, Day, Mom, Aunt, Beth, Misty 2. No, I shouldn't be surprised that her name in the telephone book is listed as Po, T. K. 3. more clearly 4. A. <u>super</u>intendent B. <u>pseudo</u>nym C. <u>multi</u>grain D. <u>poly</u>gons 5. (d) hastily 6. AMV/RA: Falling to the floor, the basket of dried flowers crumbled. A basket of dried flowers crumbled when it fell to the floor. When a basket of dried flowers fell to the floor, the flowers crumbled.

Day 89: 1. His, Belgian, Lion's, Club 2. By the way, the following streets are closed: Ash Place, Lazy Lane, and Ruby Drive. 3. well, today 4. A. jays B. donkeys C. histories D. alloys E. guppies F. lullabies 5. (c) capsizing 6. AMV/RA: Cuckoos are grayish-brown birds that lay eggs in the nests of other birds. Cuckoos, grayish-brown birds, lay their eggs in other birds' nests. Cuckoos, birds that lays their eggs in the nests of others, are grayish-brown.

Day 90: 1. We, Natchez, Trace, Parkway, Native, American 2. "If you agree," said Mrs. Leon, "please raise your hand." 3. <u>handles</u> need 4. AMV/RA: A vigorous wind blew. 5. (a) brush 6. AMV/RA: We cannot go to the park until our parents come home. We have to wait until our parents come home to go to the park. We can go to the park, but we must wait until our parents come home.

Day 91:
1.   I. Vacation tours
       A. Land
          1. Bus
          2. Train
       B. Cruises
2. Toward the end of winter, they visited their aunt in Washington, D.C. 3. A. really B. real 4. line 1: student's name; line 2: student's street address; line 3: student's city, state, and zip 5. (a) sob 6. AMV/RA: Monkey bread, the fruit of the African baobao tree, is eaten by monkeys. Monkeys eat the fruit of the African baobao tree; this fruit is referred to as monkey bread.

Day 92:
1.   Maybe he believes me, maybe not,
     Maybe I can marry him, maybe not.
2.   Miss R. Poshski
     2396 S. Chrysler Dr.
     Auburn Hills, MI 48326
3. A. <u>C</u> B. <u>A</u> C. <u>C</u> 4. any 5. (c) nudge 6. AMV/RA: The waitress from England who spoke with a British accent served muffins. The British waitress with the accent served muffins.

Day 93: 1. A. Brilliant, Britain B. Suburb, Green C. Teachers, Are, Special 2. By the end of the third quarter, both teams' coaches were shouting excitedly. 3. <u>I must have left</u> my package ~~in the car~~. direct object = package 4. A. _ B. ✓

C. _ D. ✓ E. _ F. _   **5.** (d) terrifying   **6.** AMV/RA: The child drew a picture of a house with two doors and no windows. The house in the child's drawing had two doors and no windows.

Day 94:   **1.** We, Penn's, Park, Molly   **2.** Alli, I'd like to borrow your long, silk scarf for a play.   **3.** A. ✓ B. ✓ C. _ D. ✓   **4.** A. **DC** B. **IC**   **5.** (d) cow   **6.** AMV/RA: An ostrich, a swift-running bird, is the largest and most powerful bird. An ostrich, the largest and most powerful bird, is swift-running.

Day 95:   **1.** Yesterday, Dutch, Hyde, Square, Hume, Lane   **2.** The baker answered, "No, this isn't a three-layer cake."   **3.** Monday, Kam, printer, computer   **4.** A. **P** B. **C**   **5.** (a) helicopter   **6.** AMV/RA: Moaning softly, the displeased patient waited in the doctor's office for an hour. As the displeased patient waited in the doctor's office for an hour, he moaned softly.

Day 96:   **1.** During, French, Indian, War, Iroquois, Indians, British   **2.** Dean's mother asked, "Isn't your brother twenty-nine?"   **3.** A. risen B. blown C. worn D. grown E. sunk   **4.** herself   **5.** (c) heroine   **6.** AMV/RA: Diana's antique doll has a cracked, porcelain head. Diana's antique doll has a porcelain head that is cracked.

Day 97:   **1.** Is, English, Union, South, Africa   **2.** "Brandy, you're first on my list," said Tate.   **3.** a state of being happy   **4.** good   **5.** A. ✓ B. _   **6.** AMV/RA: Although a cucumber is a vine-growing fruit with a green rind, a cucumber tree is a North American magnolia tree. A cucumber is a vine-growing fruit with a green rind; however, a cucumber tree is a North American magnolia tree.

Day 98:   **1.** Take, Interstate, Seventh, Street, Bank, One, Ballpark   **2.** Alec's sister-in-law yelled clearly, loudly, and enthusiastically during the boat race.   **3.** A. she's B. I'm C. wasn't D. can't E. couldn't F. you'll   **4.** A. **A** B. **P**   **5.** A. impurity B. natural C. spraying   **6.** AMV/RA: Looking for antique clothes for a play, Sandor was rummaging through his grandfather's old trunk. Sandor, rummaging through his grandfather's old trunk, looked for antique clothes for a play.

Day 99:   **1.** The, Dead, Sea, Middle, East   **2.** "A teachers' conference," said Dr. Oxnard, "is being organized by Mrs. D. Tang."   **3.** A. feet B. oxen C. media   **4.** any   **5.** A. troubling B. leaned C. riddled   **6.** AMV/RA: Whereas a male African elephant may grow up to thirteen feet tall, a male Asian elephant may grow up to eleven feet tall.   A male African elephant may grow up to thirteen feet tall; a male Asian elephant may grow up to eleven feet tall.

Day 100:   **1.** Pedro, Look, German, Boo   **2.** Aren, by the way, saves one-fifth of his salary.   **3.** well   **4.** A. AMV/RA: irritated, perplexed B. pedal C. AMV/RA: allow, grant   **5.** (a) entertain   **6.** AMV/RA: These tires that are almost new are very worn and dangerous.   Although these tires are almost new, they are worn and dangerous.

Day 101: 1. They, Chinese-American, Lotus, Restaurant 2. Layla's grandparents traveled to Ensenada, Mexico, by bus. 3. A. Canadian B. English C. Mexican 4. <u>Marta</u>, <u>mother drive</u>, <u>shop</u> 5. (a) friendly 6. AMV/RA: A camel's hair brush used by artists is really made from squirrels' tails.

Day 102: 1. They, Hog, Island, Virginia, Atlantic, Ocean 2. The men's swim team hasn't practiced at the Y. M. C. A. for several years. 3. A. Their B. too C. May 4. their (*Our, your*, or *my* may be accepted; however, they give different meaning to the sentence.) 5. (d) gallon 6. AMV/RA: The crying baby has a fever and an ear infection. Because the baby has a fever and an ear infection, he is crying. The baby is crying because he has a fever and an ear infection.

Day 103: 1. The, Populist, Party, American, Megan 2. A. "Amusement Park" B. "All Summer in a Day" C. <u>The Tigger Movie</u> 3. Hand me a wrench. 4. A. they're B. won't C. he'd D. I'll E. can't F. here's 5. (a) weight 6. AMV/RA: Few people know about this quiet, secluded camping spot.

Day 104: 1. Was, Jefferson, Davis, Confederate, States, America
2.   7771 Neese Road
     Woodstock, GA 30188
     April 12, 20--
Dear Andy,
  Come join our fun-filled day of balloon rides, water games, and a picnic. We hope to see you soon. (!)
     Your friend,
     Karen
3. <u>Lori tugged</u>,<u>inserted</u> 4. <u>Jacy sent</u>, D.O. = card, I.O. = Amy 5. (c) option 6. AMV/RA: Because someone had forgotten to turn off the water, our yard flooded. Our yard flooded because someone had forgotten to turn off the water.

Day 105: 1. The, Organization, American, States, Friday, Latin, American 2. Eduardo Chavez, M. D., is all of the nurses' favorite doctor. 3. A. future B. present C. past 4. A. <u>S</u> B. <u>S</u> 5. (b) pull 6. AMV/RA: Two brothers did their chores before eating lunch with their cousin at a pizzeria. Two brothers ate lunch with their cousin at a pizzeria after doing their chores.

Day 106:
1.   9555 Madison Avenue
     New York, NY 10016
     July 13, 20--
My dear cousin,
  Did you know that the Milky Way Galaxy is shaped like a spiral? We are studying it in science class.
     Your friend,
     Kino
2. "Are carp, trout, and salmon considered bony fish?" asked Mano. 3. A. heading B. greeting or salutation C. body D. closing E. signature 4. AMV/RA: **Yeah!** We're finished! 5. A. _ B. √ 6. AMV/RA: A hammerhead can refer to a

type of shark or to an African bird.   A hammerhead can refer either to a type of shark or to an African bird.

Day 107:   **1.** On, June, King, John, England, Magna, Carta   **2.** You must eat your vegetables, or you can't have pie or cake.   **3.** A. interrogative B. imperative C. declarative   **4.** silliest   **5.** (c) drought   **6.** AMV/RA: A beagle, a small hound with a smooth coat, is used for hunting.   A hunting dog, the beagle is a small hound with a smooth coat.

Day 108:   **1.** Was, Okefenoke, Swamp, Florida, Seminole, Indians
2.   I. Wind storms
         A. Hurricanes
         B. Tornadoes
      II. Snowstorms
3. and   **4.** A. <u>**C**</u> B. <u>**C**</u> C. <u>**C**</u>   **5.** (b) minister   **6.** AMV/RA: Marco and Kammi bought an Oriental screen at an estate sale. When Marco and Kammi attended an estate sale, they bought an Oriental screen.

Day 109:   **1.** Go, Dreyer, Lane, Rodrick, Stone, Company, Grandma   **2.** Ms. Stella Holuba lives in a small, rustic cottage near Frederick, Maryland.   **3.** A. √ B. √ C. _ D. _ E. √ F. √   **4.** A. **P** B. **C**   **5.** A. persuing B. tied C. shoeless   **6.** AMV/RA: This silver bracelet has turquoise insets and scroll designs. This silver bracelet with scroll designs has turquoise insets.

Day 110:   **1.** In, Janny, Christian, Jesus   **2.** A. gal. B. ft. C. blvd.   **3.** When, often, somewhere   **4.** us   **5.** (d) eternal   **6.** AMV/RA: While the toddlers played on the sandy beach, their mother sat reading a magazine under an umbrella. As the mother sat reading a magazine under an umbrella, the toddlers played on the sandy beach.

Day 111:   **1.** Are, Morgan, Willow, Mill, Farm   **2.** "You're, without a doubt, the team's best player!" exclaimed Ned.   **3.** A. driven B. drunk   **4.** A. quadruple B. octopus C. Pentagon   **5.** (d) delay   **6.** AMV/RA: Trifle, an English dessert, contains sponge cake, fruit, and whipped cream. Trifle, a dessert composed of sponge cake, fruit, and whipped cream, is an English dessert.

Day 112:   **1.** Wave, Hill, Mansion, Hudson, River, New, York's, Bronx   **2.** "Aren't we appealing the decision, Mr Bodnar?" asked his client.   **3.** myself   **4.** <u>son bought</u>; I.O. = them; D.O. = bookcase.   **5.** (d) idea   **6.** AMV/RA: The coral snake, a small, poisonous one, is related to the cobra. The small, poisonous coral snake is related to the cobra.

Day 113:   **1.** The, Japanese, Dazel, Company, Eagle, Express   **2.** My mother's cousin came to visit from Dublin, Ireland, last fall.   **3.** A. _ B. √   **4.** <u>company must have sent</u>; D.O. = order   **5.** A. fretting B. hollered C. hammering   **6.** AMV/RA: Both Lida and her best friend, Jemima, are quiet and shy.

Day 114: 1. From, A. D., European, Middle, Ages
2.
                    13 Bond Street
                    London, England
                    May 20, 20--
Dear Madison,
    I'm sending the book entitled <u>Angel Unaware</u>.
                  Love,
                  Pam

3. AMV/RA: Wow!
4.
do	may	shall	was
does	might	will	were
did	must	can	be
has	should	is	being
have	could	am	been
had	would	are	

5. A. cantoring   B. scrubbed   C. rapidly   6. AMV/RA: A peanut is a legume whose pod grows underground. The pod of a peanut, which is a legume, grows underground.

DAY 115:
1.
                    73354 Harrison Street
                    Topeka, KS 66603
                    November 2, 20--

Dear Trevor,
    Would you like to go to the Pacific Northwest with us?
                  My regards,
                  Josh

2. "I believe," said Ramon, "that you're leaving at 3:15."
3. A. heading B. greeting or salutation C. body D. closing E. signature
4. <u>x</u>, <u>sh</u>, <u>s</u>, <u>ch</u>, <u>z</u>   5. (a) offensive   6. AMV/RA: After Aleta's first reaction of panic, she sat down and closed her eyes. Aleta's first reaction was panic; however, she sat down and closed her eyes. Although Aleta's first reaction was panic, she sat down and closed her eyes.

Day 116:
1. I. Books
    A. Mysteries
        1. Fiction
        2. Nonfiction
    B. Historical romances
  II. Magazines

2. The M. C. Kraft Co. has moved to 33 Trellis Dr., St. Louis, Missouri.   3. me   4. March, Tessa, Boston, train   5. (c) alligator   6. AMV/RA: Sir Arthur Conan Doyle was an English physician and novelist who wrote Sherlock Holmes stories. Sir Arthur Conan Doyle, the author of Sherlock Holmes stories, was an English physician and novelist.

Day 117: **1.** The, Jackson, Historical, Society, Sunday, Caledonia, State, Park, May **2.** During John F. Kennedy's presidency, many Americans joined the Peace Corp. **3.** most noisily **4.** A. doesn't B. you're **5.** (a) temperature **6.** AMV/RA: Our picnic that has been canceled due to rain has been scheduled for next week.

Day 118: **1.** The, Phoenix, Suns, Memorial, Coliseum **2.** Elizabeth asked, "Haven't you been to Madrid, Spain, in the summer?" **3.** A. **C** B. **A** C. **A** **4.** line 1: student's name; line 2: student's street address; line 3: student's city, state, and zip code **5.** (b) granite **6.** AMV/RA: Abbie had her picture taken at a pillory in historic Williamsburg, Virginia.

Day 119: **1.** Last, Judge, Wing, Lightner, Museum, Spanish, St., Augustine **2.** Chessa and Don lived in Lake Tahoe, Nevada, for twenty-one years. **3.** an object that is carved **4.** AMV/RA: Is your Siamese cat ill? **5.** (c) starving **6.** AMV/RA: An oval ball used in Rugby football may be passed, carried, or dribbled with the feet.

Day 120: **1.** In, Mendel's **2.** Mr. Cord, her kindergarten teacher, spoke at a volunteers' luncheon. (or) Mr. Cord, her kindergarten teacher spoke at a volunteers' luncheon. **3.** A. their B. really C. Too D. they're **4.** A. √ B. _ C. _ D. √ E. _ F. √ **5.** (d) protection **6.** AMV/RA: Mrs. Hanson inherited a 1935 car, but it won't start. The 1935 car that Mrs. Hanson inherited won't start.

Day 121: **1.** The, Federalist, Party, Alexander, Hamilton, Washington, D., C.
2.
           1 S. Stratton Street
           Gettysburg, PA 17325
           May 20, 20--
Dear Gregg,
    The boys' wrestling team from our high school will compete next week in Durango, Colorado.
           Your friend,
           Paco
3. A. really B. well **4.** woman, castle, tour, moat, dungeon, tower **5.** (d) sunset **6.** AMV/RA: Elba, a small Italian island in the Tyrrhenian Sea, was the site of Napoleon's exile. Elba, the site of Napoleon's exile, is a small Italian island in the Tyrrhenian Sea.

Day 122: **1.** Has, Aunt, Nicole, Princess, Birds, Bears, Miracle, Market, Tenth, Street **2.** Mr. Gore's silk, flowered tie with tropical birds looked great with his three-piece suit. **3.** <u>dog</u>, <u>cats</u> <u>like</u> **4.** enormous (milkshakes), chocolate (milkshakes), chicken (sandwiches) **5.** A. _ B. √ **6.** AMV/RA: His grandfather who was a soldier in World War II was part of the famous Normandy Invasion. His grandfather, a soldier in World War II, was part of the famous Normandy Invasion.

Day 123: **1.** A. Teen, Angel B. Out, Wilderness C. The, Back, Page **2.** The book entitled <u>Two Pennies for Parker</u> was a short, funny novel. **3.** A. present B.

past C. future   4. A. _ B. √ C. _ D. √   5. (a) plant   6. AMV/RA: Sarah is a journalist whose article about saving whales won an award.   Sarah who is a journalist wrote an award-winning article about saving whales.

Day 124:   1. A, Vicksburg, Civil, War   2. The producer, the director, and the script writer discussed the movie's length.   3. A. **P** B. **A**   4. merchant, mercy, noisy, nosy, notary, practice, prance   5. A. canning B. caning C. hibernation   6. AMV/RA: Pago Pago is a seaport on Tutuila Island, part of American Samoa.

Day 125:   1. At, Alpine, German, Restaurant, Austrian   2. Her foot was badly sprained, and she was taken to her doctor's office.   3. A. aren't B. I'll C. wouldn't D. where's E. won't F. we're   4. good   5. A. √ B. _   6. AMV/RA: Ben Franklin, the peacemaker at the Constitutional Convention, later became the first Postmaster General of the United States.   Ben Franklin was the peacemaker at the Constitutional Convention; he later became the first Postmaster General of the United States.

Day 126:   1. The, Alabama, Gulf, Mexico   2. Yes, Dan, they live at the base of those high, snow-covered peaks.   3. himself   4. characterized by glamour   5. A. √ B. _   6. AMV/RA: While some children are sledding, others are building a snowman.   Some children are sledding; others are building a snowman.

Day 127:   1. Have, Lars, Waterpocket, Canyon, Utah   2. A. "Visions in Charcoal" B. "A Butterfly for Parkie" C. <u>Air Force 1</u>   3. <u>One</u>, is   4. two ministers' office   5. (b) dry   6. AMV/RA: Alicia's brother and sister ate all of the chocolate chip cookies that she had just baked.

Day 128:   1. Is, Castle, Chillon, Lake, Leman, Swiss, Alps, Europe   2. Pippa's name, if I'm correct, was listed alphabetically as Swesey, Pippa.   3. A. **F** B. **S**   4. A. moos B. tomatoes C. egos   5. (d) crucial   6. AMV/RA: Ludwig Mies designed a Chicago house built on steel piers.   A Chicago house built on on steel piers was designed by Ludwig Mies.

Day 129:   1. Is, Mt., Elbert, Colorado's, Sawatch, Mountains   2. Peppy and smiling, several cheerleaders ran onto the stage.   3. A. **IC** B. **DC**   4. A. AMV/RA: flexible B. AMV/RA: rigid   5. (b) pound   6. AMV/RA: The flying fox is a type of fruit-eating bat that lives in Africa, Asia, and Australia.   The flying fox, a type of bat that eats fruit, is indigenous to Africa, Asia, and Australia.

Day 130:   1. In, I, African   2. A. "Back from Mars" B. <u>Camping Life</u> C. "Vertebrates"   3. good   4. brothers' inn   5. (d) diminutive   6. AMV/RA: William Henry Harrison, the ninth President of the United States, was called Tippecanoe.

Day 131:   1. My, Jo, Chester, County, Brandywine, Valley   2. Mrs. Uman makes baskets; you'll find them at craft shows at the M. T. A. building.   3. carefully, within

4. A. *micro*organisms B. *semi*circle C. *post*script. D. *trans*ports
5. A. casualty B. caring C. careful D. rarity   **6.** AMV/RA: The boy tripped over a garden hose, fell on a wooden walkway, and broke his arm. When the boy tripped over a garden hose and fell on a wooden walkway, he broke his arm.

Day 132:   **1.**   My, I, Negro, Swing, Low, Sweet, Chariot   **2.** Dad needs the following: flour, one-third cup of sugar, and apples.   **3.** A. **C** B. **P**   **4.** A. Alaskan B. Spanish C. Greek   **5. (a)** car   **6.** AMV/RA: The laughing children are watching a puppet show. The children who are watching a puppet show are laughing.

Day 133:
1.
                                            12 **N**orth 56th **S**treet
                                            Orange **P**ark, **FL** 32073
                                            June 2, 20--
    Dear **M**rs. **L**una,
        My mother received the **L**ifetime **A**chievement **A**ward from a service club in **R**aleigh, **N**orth **C**arolina.
                                             Sincerely,
                                             Jolene

2. Stuck in traffic, the taxi driver looked for a faster, quicker route.   **3.** <u>Frank, John,</u> and <u>I are going</u>   **4.** building.   **5. (d)** century   **6.** AMV/RA: A seahorse is a semitropical fish that normally swims in an upright position. A seahorse, a semitropical fish, normally swims in an upright position.

Day 134:
1. I. American life
      A. Colonial times
      B. Modern times
  II. British life
2. No, their grandparents twenty-fifth anniversary wasn't celebrated on Dec. 16, 2000.
3. antic, antler, attic, cattle, deal, deem   **4.** A. stolen B. frozen C. taken D. saw E. eaten   **5.** A. stirred B. freezing C. sweetly D. annoyed   **6.** AMV/RA: The couple visited Oatlands Plantation, an 1803 mansion in the South.

Day 135:   **1.** The, William, Chase, Society, Painters, Pastel   **2.** Happy and excited, the children loaded the bus.   **3.** <u>(You)</u> Put   **4.** AMV/RA: The Tropic of Cancer is north of the equator.   **5. (b)** Antarctica   **6.** AMV/RA: The upset woman was searching the neighborhood for her lost poodle. The upset woman whose poodle was lost searched the neighborhood for him.

Day 136:   **1.** In, June, Democratic, Party, New, York, City   **2.** Our principal, Tom Nast, makes short, snappy speeches.   **3.** conj. = and; intj. = Whoa!   **4.** most unusual   **5. (d)** herbal   **6.** AMV/RA: The kitchen floor is caked with mud and needs to be washed. Because the kitchen floor is caked with mud, it needs to be washed.

Day 137: 1. Samuel, Chase, American, Revolutionary, U., S., Supreme, Court
2. Mr. Greene said, "Fifty-five people attended our horse lovers' picnic."
3. AMV/RA: Bonnie, Baltimore   4. not poisonous   5. A. eroding   B. flapped
C. discreetly   D. supplied   6. AMV/RA: The Gulf Stream is a warm ocean current that flows from the Gulf of Mexico.   The Gulf Stream, a warm ocean current, flows from the Gulf of Mexico.

Day 138: 1. The, French, La, Salle, Mississippi, Valley, Louisiana, King, Louis
2. Juanita's sister visited her mother-in-law in Lisbon, Portugal, last spring.
3. us   4. Will their mother let them go sledding in the afternoon?   5. (d) lava
6. AMV/RA: A rabbit-shaped ceramic cup is for sale in a Victorian shop.   A ceramic cup which is shaped like a rabbit is for sale in a Victorian shop.

Day 139: 1. Green, Lake, Road, St., George, Utah, August, Dear, Deka
2. Jason Dill, our neighbor, restores antique furniture.   3. A. heading   B. greeting or salutation   4. A. **P**   B. **A**   5. (d) instruction   6. AMV/RA: Paisley is both a colorful cloth pattern and a city in Scotland.   Paisley, a colorful cloth pattern, is also a city in Scotland.

Day 140:
1. The hippopotamus is strong
   And huge of head and broad of bustle;
2. A. cm   B. c.   C. pres.   3. A. **P**   B. **C**   4. ladies' Arabian horses   5. A. delaying   B. adorable   C. starring   D. tasteless   6. AMV/RA: Haleakala National Park is a dormant volcano on Maui, an island of Hawaii.

Day 141: 1. When, Nick, I, Castaway's   2. The cabin in the pines is isolated; we'll need to take supplies.   3. driver, passenger was   4. aside, reluctantly, suddenly, down   5. (a) pound   6. AMV/RA: An echidna is a spine-covered, toothless mammal that eats ants with its sticky tongue.   Spine-covered and toothless, the echidna eats ants with its sticky tongue.

Day 142: 1. The, Greek, Homer, B., C.   2. Bought by a racer, the car was low to the ground, sleek, and fast.   3. Have you seen; D.O. = jacket   4. A. boy's dog
B. boys' dog   5. A. consumable   B. rechargeable   C. lovable   6. AMV/RA: Whereas haute couture is the designing of ladies' high fashion, haute cuisine is the preparing of fine foods.   Haute couture is the designing of ladies' high fashion, but haute cuisine is the preparing of fine foods.

Day 143: 1. Is, Canadian, Remembrance, Day, November, American, Veteran's, Day   2. Kala, Jose, and she participated in the last event, a three-legged race.
3. anybody   4.   Student's name
   Student's street address
   City, State   Zip Code

   Kim Tsosie
   11542 North Third Street
   Philadelphia, PA   19106

5. A. relatively B. negative C. placement   **6.** AMV/RA: Joel receives an allowance, but he earns extra money by mowing his neighbors' lawns. Although Joel receives an allowance, he earns extra money by mowing his neighbors' lawns.

Day 144:   **1.** Jill, Jacy's, Justine, Drive, Colorado, Springs, Colorado   **2.** After a very long introduction, Carol Tang, R. N., spoke at the nurses' conference.
3.
do	may	shall	was
does	might	will	were
did	must	can	be
has	should	is	being
have	could	am	been
had	would	are	

4. bravery, knight, king, country   **5.** (b) proud   **6.** AMV/RA: Their cocker spaniel has a long, shaggy coat and long ears. Their dog, a cocker spaniel, has a long, shaggy coat and long ears.

Day 145:   **1.** We, Thomas, Point, Lighthouse, Chesapeake, Bay, Annapolis
2.
```
                          3 E. King St.
                          Shippensburg, PA  17257
                          Oct. 23, 20--
Dear Aren,
    I've bought a home in Brussels, Belgium.  Let's get
together to talk about it.
                          Friends forever,
                          Mary Rose
```
3. A. heading B. greeting or salutation C. body D. closing E. signature
4. AMV/RA: milk, stream   **5.** (c) altitude   **6.** AMV/RA: During their vacation to Maine, his parents visited St. John Valley and its many potato farms.

Day 146:   **1.** This, Clayton, School, Arctic, Airlines
2. Waiting for a shuttle bus, the travelers eagerly discussed the group's plan for cooking out.   **3.** A. **F** B. **R-O**   **4.** farthest   **5.** (d) garland   **6.** AMV/RA: When a door slammed, his dog became frightened and hid under the bed.

Day 147:   **1.** At, Silver, Heels, My, Friend, Life   **2.** Standing in line, the lady read a book called <u>Herbal Cooking</u>.   **3.** I, he, she, we, they, you, it (or *who*)   **4.** The woman answered in a childlike voice.   **5.** (b) canyon   **6.** AM V/RA: The teenager opened the refrigerator and took out cold meat, mustard, lettuce, and tomatoes. Opening the refrigerator, the teenager took out cold meat, mustard, lettuce, and tomatoes.

Day 148:   **1.** Last, Torres, Aspen, Thanksgiving   **2.** The class of '99 held its reunion; many couldn't attend.   **3.** A. AMV/RA: plan B. AMV/RA: open, obvious   **4.** A. well B. really   **5.** (c) serious   **6.** AMV/RA: Making an ice cream float, Lani poured root beer into a tall glass and added vanilla ice cream. When Lani made an ice cream float, she poured root beer into a tall glass and added vanilla ice cream.

Day 149: **1.** Whose woods these are I think I know,
His house is in the village though,
2. Did you, Carlo, become seasick due to the swirling, choppy sea? **3.** A. growled B. will present C. takes **4.** friendliest **5.** A. <u>C</u> B. <u>S</u> **6.** AMV/RA: Although Tessa will sell tickets for the medieval fair, she cannot attend. Tessa will sell tickets for the medieval fair, but she cannot attend.

Day 150: **1.** In, I, President, John, F., Kennedy, Peace, Corps, Americans **2.** A. "Good Morning to You" B. <u>Wallace and Ladmo</u> C. <u>The ABC's of Hawaii</u> **3.** A. <u>ADV.</u> B. <u>ADJ.</u> **4.** A. _ B. _ C. _ D. ✓ **5.** (b) friend **6.** AMV/RA: A starfish has five arms arranged like the points of a star, and a starflower is a white or pink five-petaled, star-shaped flower.

Day 151: **1.** Hanover, Methodist, Church, Reverend, Ron, Boyd, Sunday **2.** Pippi did well on her algebra test; she's been asked to tutor other students. **3.** A. run B. taught C. broken D. lain E. thrown **4.** brass, antique, small, hand-carved, cherry **5.** (c) clamp **6.** AMV/RA: Located at the tip of South America, Cape Horn is known for its strong currents and its stormy weather. Cape Horn, which is located at the tip of South America, is known for its strong currents and stormy weather.

Day 152: **1.** A. Home, Range B. As, Time, Goes, By C. More, Is, Less **2.** Her name was listed in the commencement program as Ramos, Misty S. **3.** A. ✓ B. _ C. ✓ D. ✓ E. _ F. _ G. _ H. ✓ **4.** A. it's B. don't C. you've D. I'd E. mightn't F. you're **5.** (a) sadly **6.** AMV/RA: Trichinosis is a disease that someone can get from eating improperly cooked pork.

Day 153: **1.** What, Frog, Legs, Festival, Florida, Ria **2.** A. <u>Kristina Regina</u> B. "Hey Diddle Diddle" C. "Home Is Where the Art Is" **3.** <u>I must have given</u>; D.O. = card, I.O. = brother **4.** A. <u>A</u> B. <u>A</u> **5.** A. adventurous B. solely C. stunning D. purified **6.** AMV/RA: A whelk is a large marine snail that eats crab and lobster. A whelk, a large marine snail, eats lobster and crab.

Day 154: **1.** Did, Harney, Country, Carnival **2.** A women's club meeting was held at 1201 E. Clay Street, Richmond, Virginia. **3.** themselves **4.** Two (puppies), frisky (puppies), a (hound), gray (hound), the (meadow), muddy (meadow), tree-lined (meadow) **5.** A compound sentence must have two independent clauses (complete thoughts). **6.** AMV/RA: Mr. Davis, a businessman, ordered a briefcase, business cards, and an answering machine.

Day 155: **1.** The, Is, Miss, Jordan, Department, Energy **2.** A. <u>In the Stoneworks</u> B. <u>Good Morning, World</u> C. "Aging Kitties" **3.** A. Russ's toys B. brothers' cupcakes **4.** A. <u>un</u>related B. <u>im</u>penetrable C. <u>il</u>literate D. <u>non</u>toxic E. <u>in</u>coherent **5.** (b) theft **6.** AMV/RA: Marco's aunt and uncle from Iowa attended a family reunion held at South Mountain Fairgrounds. The family reunion attended by Marco's aunt and uncle was held at South Mountain Fairgrounds.

Day 156: **1.** Lulu, My, Pacific, Northwest, Seattle **2.** Loni, his brother's girlfriend, will be arriving at 4:00 P. M. *or* Loni, his brother's girlfriend will be arriving at 4:00 P. M. **3.** A. No B. before C. tri (or *multi*) **4.** most carefully **5.** (b) inform **6.** AMV/RA: Living off the Indian Ocean, the dugong is a large tropical mammal that feeds mostly on seaweed. A dugong is a tropical mammal that lives off the Indian Ocean and feeds mostly on seaweed.

Day 157: **1.** In, United, States, Congress, House, Representatives **2.** "My first grandchild," said Sen. Smith proudly, "was born on Monday, January 1, 2001." **3.** A. <u>C</u> B. <u>C</u> **4.** line 1: student's name; line 2: student's street address; line 3: student's city, state   zip code **5.** (a) hostile **6.** AMV/RA: Because hail the size of marbles pelted our vehicle, we pulled off the road. We pulled off the road because hail the size of marbles pelted our vehicle.

Day 158: **1.** Did, Abraham, Lincoln, Emancipation, Proclamation, Anderson, House **2.** Yes, our canoe trip is Friday; we want you to come, Cole. **3.** <u>One leaned</u>, <u>grabbed</u> **4.** A. a church's craft show B. men's basketball team C. chefs' pastries **5.** A. striped B. stripped C. relying D. reliable **6.** AMV/RA: The 1956 ranch-style house has been restored. The ranch-style house that was built in 1956 has been restored.

Day 159: **1.** Grandpa, Ngi, Traveling, During, Winter, Traveler's, Digest **2.** "Jennifer, will you go with me to Cody, Wyoming, sometime?" asked Polly. **3.** AMV/RA: Sit down. **4.** A. <u>DC</u> B. <u>IC</u> **5.** (d) heart **6.** AMV/RA: When the class voted and decided to take an essay test, some students were perturbed. Some students were perturbed because the class voted to take an essay test.

Day 160: **1.** Is, Hoover, Dam, Colorado, River, Nevada **2.** His reply, without a doubt, surprised Randy, his dad, and his mother. **3.** he **4.** quickly **5.** (a) goose **6.** AMV/RA: The gorilla, the largest and most powerful ape, is native to African jungles. The gorilla which is the largest and most powerful ape is native to African jungles.

Day 161: **1.** With, Jefferson's, Louisiana, Purchase, America, Mississippi, River, Rocky, Mountains **2.** After the Memorial Day parade, we're staying with you until 4:00, Trisha. **3.** so, softly, not, well **4.** A. <u>F</u> B. <u>R-O</u> C. <u>S</u> **5.** (a) attentively **6.** AMV/RA: When an enormous black bug scurried across the floor, everyone left the room. As an enormous black bug scurried across the floor, everyone left the room.

Day 162: **1.** Her, Hill, Country, Club, Halloween
2. I. Patterns
　　A. Geometric
　　B. Spiral
　II. Blueprints
3. A. German B. Irish C. European **4.** AMV/RA: The sentence should contain *and, but, or.* **5.** (c) pottery **6.** AMV/RA: Our plans for next Friday are to visit an art museum or a science museum. Our plans for next Friday are to visit an art

museum; however, we may visit a science museum rather than an art museum.

Day 163: **1./2.**
                           2 **N**. Michigan Ave.
                           Chicago, **IL**
                           Nov. 29, 20--
Dear Wes,
    Our family went to the **M**useum of **N**orthern **A**rizona last summer. **W**e learned that early **I**ndians of **A**rizona had turkeys and dogs as domesticated animals.
                           Your cousin,
                           Rosa

3. A. heading B. greeting or salutation C. body D. closing E. signature **4.** AMV/RA: *Whoa!* Let's slow down! **5.** A. atrophied B. discerning C. easement **6.** AMV/RA: A koala, a tree-dwelling Australian animal, feeds exclusively on eucalyptus leaves and buds. A koala is a tree-dwelling Australian animal that feeds exclusively on eucalyptus leaves and buds.

Day 164:
1. I. Plant cell
     A. Nucleus
     B. Chloroplasts
  II. Animal cell

2. Pat Mahlan, master of ceremonies, handed Nicole Yassi, D. A., the award. **3.** A. surprised B. lives C. will be **4.** AMV/RA: Video - a tape that one watches **5.** **(c)** peninsula **6.** AMV/RA: After examining the patient, a poodle, Dr. Jones wrote a prescription. Dr. Jones examined the poodle and wrote a prescription.

Day 165: **1.** Last, Mayor, Troon, St., Patrick's, Day
2.
                           12893 W. Summit Hill Dr.
                           Knoxville, TN 37902
                           February 28, 2001

Dear Aleta,
    Peter is now twenty-one years old.(!) It's hard to believe that my talkative, energetic toddler grew up so quickly.(!)
                           Yours truly,
                           Marcy

3. most frightened **4.** (d) shrewd **5.** A. lovely B. succeeded C. omitting D. refusal **6.** AMV/RA: The sterling pin which she inherited from her grandmother has many tiny pearls around its edge. *Note:* Placing commas before and after *which she inherited from her grandmother* is also acceptable.

Day 166: **1.** In, October, John, Singer, Sargent, Chicago, Museum, Art **2.** Wow! Lu has moved to 1 Easy Street, Carefree, Arizona, and she has seen a scorpion! **3.** A. AMV/RA: pond, officer, tent B. AMV/RA: Red River, Corbin, America C. AMV/RA: letter, rake, tank D. AMV/RA: trust, beauty, wish **4.** That (home), new (home), model (home), tall (doors), French (doors), a (counter), granite (counter), kitchen (counter) **5.** (a) modify **6.** AMV/RA: A redingote is a long, full-skirted coat that opens down the front.   Long and full-skirted, a redingote is a coat that is open down the front.

Day 167:   **1.** The, Kalish, Chihuahuan, Desert, Arizona   **2.** Yes, we'll go to Montezuma's Castle, my friend.   **3.** AMV/RA: We're allowed to go!   **4.** <u>Mrs. Lu hugged</u>; direct objects = Rebecca, me   **5.** A. forgetting B. beginner C. forgetful
6. AMV/RA: After dinner, Molly always rinses the plates while Melissa and Scott put leftovers in the refrigerator.

Day 168:   **1.** The, Communist, Party, Vladimir, Lenin, Russia   **2.** Your souvenir, the small, wooden carving, will be your mother's favorite gift.   **3.** A. √ B. _
4. line 1: street address; line 2: city, state zip code; line 3: today's date   **5.** A. excellent B. sauciness C. pitying   **6.** AMV/RA: The hostess welcomed the guest and introduced him to others at the gathering.   Having welcomed the guest, the hostess introduced him to others at the gathering.   After welcoming the guest, the hostess introduced him to others at the gathering.

Day 169:   **1.** Several, Jewish, Jerusalem, Passover   **2.** One-fifth of the class must bring the following for the craft: yarn, pine cones, but-tons, and paint.   **3.** A. Tara's pearls B. cities' problems C. women's opinion   **4.** pardon, pride, prim, pristine, quake, quiet   **5. (c)** label   **6.** AMV/RA: Erupting in 79 A. D., Mt. Vesuvius, a volcano on the Bay of Naples, destroyed Pompeii, Italy.   Mt. Vesuvius, a volcano on the Bay of Naples, erupted in 79 A. D. and destroyed Pompeii, Italy.

Day 170:   **1.** A, Greek, Richard, British   **2.** A. km B. lb. C. oz.   **3.** <u>grandparents</u>, <u>father</u> <u>volunteers</u>   **4.** AMV/RA: truth, loyalty, honesty   **5. (d)** rebel
6. AMV/RA: To make pickled eggs, Dad cooks the eggs, peels them, and places them in beet juice.

Day 171:   **1.** A. A, Big, Mistake B. A, Look, Future C. Much, Ado, About, Nothing
2. Tina said, "You've heard, of course, that he's moving."   **3.** A. <u>Kim could have come</u> B. <u>balloon has burst</u> C. <u>I should have known</u> D. <u>Josh Has beaten</u>
E. <u>juror has been sworn</u>   **4.** A. <u>P</u> B. <u>C</u>   **5.** A. disgraceful B. recurring
C. denial D. strapped   **6.** AMV/RA: Asian warriors invented the leather saddle 2,000 years ago.   The leather saddle was invented by Asian warriors 2,000 years ago.

Day 172:   **1.** Samuel, Champlain, Frenchman, Fort, Quebec, Canada
2.   12507 N. 67th St.
                                         Scottsdale, AZ 85254
                                         June 1, 20--
Dear Mano,
     We arrived at two o'clock last Thursday, May 7. Let's meet next week at my aunt's house on Elkton Ridge.
                                         Always,
                                         Lanzo
3. A. <u>√</u> B. _ C. <u>√</u> D. _   **4.** most closely   **5. (d)** fuse   **6.** AMV/RA:

Silver balls hang on the gigantic department store's Christmas tree.   The gigantic Christmas tree in the department store is decorated with silver balls.

Day 173:   1. Is, Triangle, X, Ranch, Grand, Teton, National, Park, Jackson, Wyoming   2. Yes, those ladies' holiday plans, most definitely, must be considered.   3. a heart specialist   4. A. children   B. cliffs   C. trophies   D. pitches   E. centipedes   F. sheep   G. mysteries   H. atlases   5. (d) cattle   6. AMV/RA: The team followed the cheerleaders who ran onto the field waving their pompoms.   Ten cheerleaders waved their pompoms and ran onto the football field as the team followed them.

Day 174:   1. Are, Hausa, Nigeria, Islamic   2. Our Mexican food was hot -- extremely hot. (!)   3. A. √ writers' conference   B. √ men's club
4. your name
your street address
your city, state   zip code
                Lou Mariana
                2 Moanalua Freeway
                Honolulu, Hawaii   96819
5. A. amusement   B. written   C. applied   6. AMV/RA: Craig's neighbors rode in the Chunnel from London to Paris during their vacation.   When Craig's neighbors were on their vacation, they rode in the Chunnel from London to Paris.

Day 175:   1. During, World, War, Americans, Europe, Allies'   2. Their television was loud -- too loud for me. or Their television was loud (too loud for me). (!)   3. A. well   B. really   4. A. ! exclamatory   B. ? interrogative   C. . declarative   D. . imperative   5. (c) person   6. AMV/RA: Thomas Kuykendall, an artist famous for his duck carvings, begins each duck with a block of wood.   Thomas Kuykendall who is an artist famous for his duck carvings begins each duck with a block of wood.

Day 176:   1. Located, Tanzania, Mt., Kilimanjaro, Africa   2. "I think," said Debra, "that Hampton, Virginia, was started by Jamestown colonists."   3. (c) compulsory   4. street address; city, state and zip code   5. (d) bubbly   6. AMV/RA: Jackson, Parker's cat with a gentle disposition, weighs over twenty pounds.   Jackson, Parker's cat that weighs over twenty pounds, has a gentle disposition.

Day 177:   1. He, The, Midnight, Ride, Paul, Revere, Independence, Day
2. "This recipe, I believe, calls for self-rising flour," said Sharon.   3. Bonnie, patience, gossip, comments.   4. A. away from a place or situation   B. below zero   C. work together   5. A. precision   B. rallied   C. expelled   D. rallying   6. AMV/RA: Wessex, a former Anglo-Saxon kingdom of Great Britain, is the setting for Thomas Hardy's novels. The setting for Thomas Hardy's novels is Wessex, a former Anglo-Saxon kingdom of Great Britain.

Day 178:
1. The world is too much with us, late and soon,
   Getting and spending, we lay waste our powers:
2. "That picture," said Tate, "was done by Norman Rockwell, a famous American artist."   3. A. <u>waiter had brought</u>   B. <u>Mom has gone</u>   C. <u>child was sitting</u>   D. <u>you Have drunk</u>   E. <u>I must have run</u>   4. more reasonable   5. (a) fertile
6. AMV/RA: Dr. Ferdinand Porsche designed the Volkswagen Beetle which was built in Germany in the 1930's. The Volkswagen Beetle which was built in Germany in the 1930's was designed by Dr. Ferdinand Porsche.

Day 179:   1. This, Victorian, Alicia, Mary, Queen, Scots   2. A. <u>Poor Little Rich Girl</u>   B. <u>Hawk Hunter</u>   C. "Comparing Haiku with Other Poetry"   3. me   4. AMV/RA: I *shall go.* Tara *will sing* solo.   5. AMV/RA: Martin likes spinach, but he detests green beans.   6. AMV/RA: Her toes that were once frostbitten become cold quickly. Her toes become cold quickly because they were once frostbitten.

Day 180:   1. On, Labor, Day, Orlando, Regency, Center   2. A men's reading group is forming; its first meeting will be next Thursday, June 1.   3. <u>company has sent</u>, D.O. = tablets, I.O. = parents   4. A. <u>**S**</u>   B. <u>**R-O**</u>   C. <u>**F**</u>   5. (a) stratus
6. AMV/RA: Amphibians, cold-blooded animals, have lungs and moist, hairless skin. Amphibians are cold-blooded animals with lungs and moist, hairless skin.